LIFE PICTURE PUZZLE

WELCOME TO LIFE'S NEW PICTURE PUZZLE BOOK

When LIFE published the original Picture Puzzle book last year, we suspected there were a lot of puzzle fans out there. We just didn't know how many. That book quickly crept onto the best-seller lists. And then it stayed there. Next thing we knew, it was No. 1.

Once their wrist cramps had subsided, puzzle fanatics began gleefully firing off letters and e-mails asking when they could expect the sequel. Well, here it is, our second LIFE Picture Puzzle book. We think you'll find it even more fun than the first. We've made a few improvements, adding 32 pages and printing the puzzles at a larger size. (So, please, no more complaints about breakfast-table wagers lost because an eagle-eyed granddaughter spotted something across her Cheerios.) We've also included two new types of puzzles, just to keep you on your toes. Our Cut-Ups will test your skill at unscrambling a photo that we've clipped into pieces and then shuffled around. To create our new LIFE Classic Puzzles, we dipped into LIFE's world-famous photo archives of thousands of great black-and-white images. You might even recognize one or two old favorites.

We're already working on a third and a fourth Picture Puzzle book. In the meantime, you can find a new puzzle each week on the back page of LIFE in your local newspaper. You can also dig into a mountain of puzzles online at *www.LIFE.com*, where you'll be seeing a few big surprises in the months ahead. And if you want to let us know what you think of the new book, drop us a line at picturepuzzle@life.com. We'd love to hear from you.

[OUR NEW CUT-UP PUZZLES: EASY AS 1-2-3]

We snipped a photo into 4, 6, 9, 12, or 16 pieces. Then we rearranged the pieces and numbered them.

Your mission: Beneath each Cut-Up, write the number of the piece in the box where it belongs.

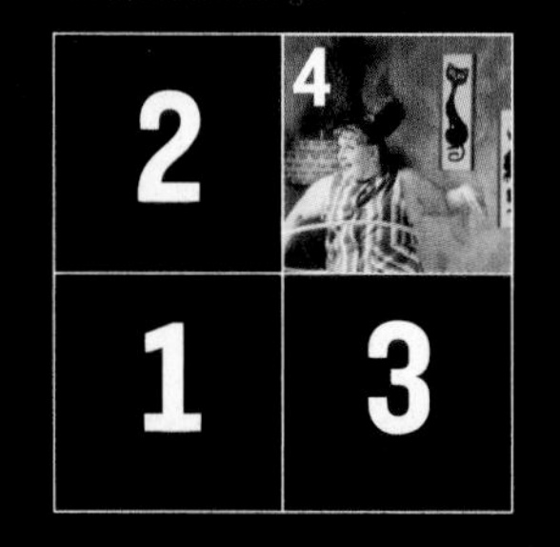

Check the answer key at the back of the book to see what the reassembled image looks like.

Secret puzzle bonus! We've concealed 10 secret changes in the puzzles within this book. Think you've found one? Log on to *www.LIFE.com/Life/extra_answers* to find out! In addition, we've hidden two more puzzles on our Web site, but you can reach them only through the private entrance: Go to *www.LIFE.com*, and click PICTURE PUZZLE. On the next page, click the second *Z* in the word PUZZLE, close your eyes, count to three, and *voilà*!

[HOW TO PLAY THE PUZZLES]

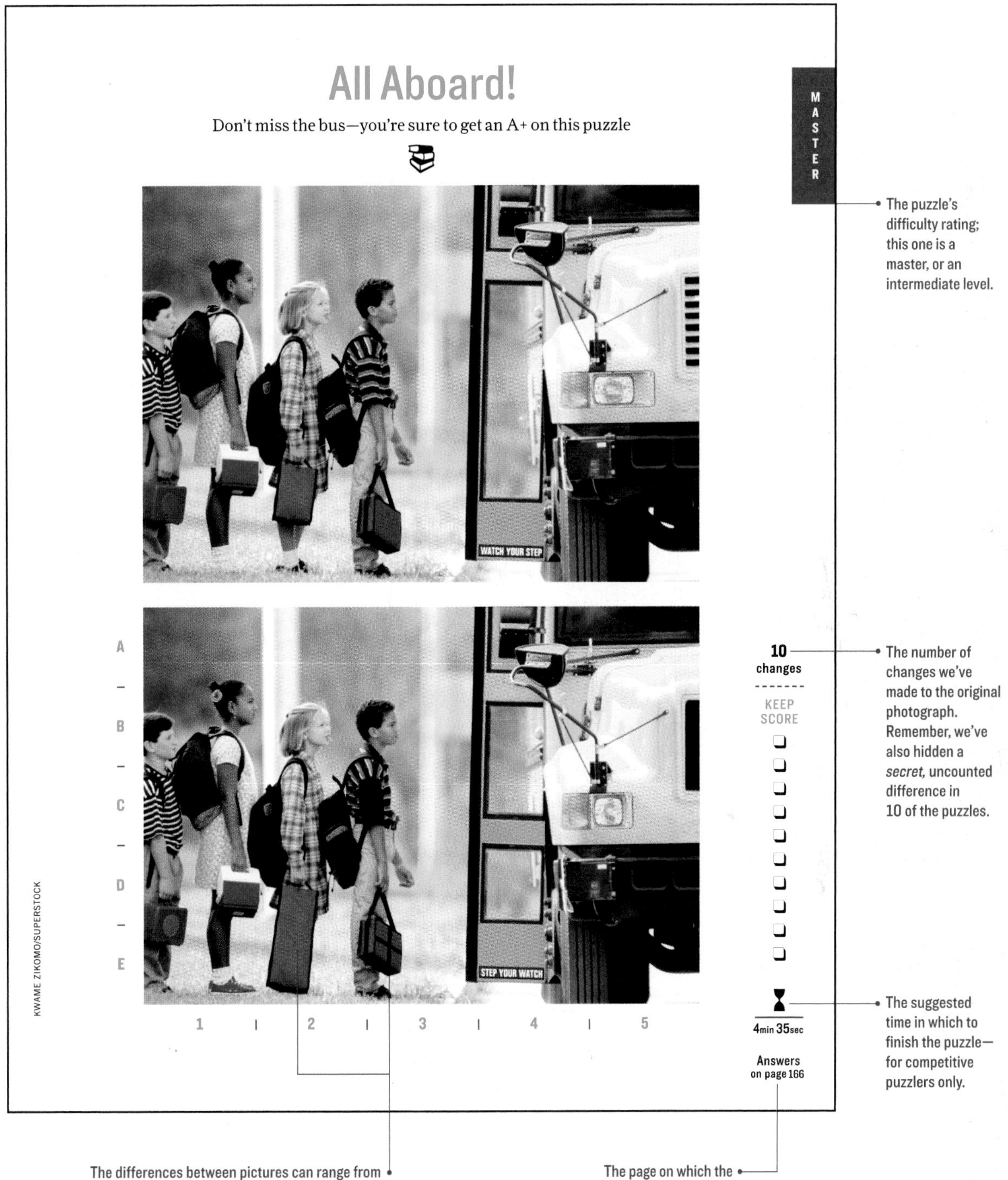

The puzzle's difficulty rating; this one is a master, or an intermediate level.

The number of changes we've made to the original photograph. Remember, we've also hidden a *secret*, uncounted difference in 10 of the puzzles.

The suggested time in which to finish the puzzle—for competitive puzzlers only.

The differences between pictures can range from the relatively obvious to the maddeningly subtle, depending on the difficulty rating. For instance, here, the girl's red bag is much bigger than it used to be, and there is a pair of extra straps on his blue bag. Eight more changes are left to spot in this one.

The page on which the answers can be found. Use the numbered and lettered grid to help you find any changes you might have missed.

LIFE PICTURE PUZZLE

Editor Mark Adams
Copy Chief Danielle Dowling
Production Manager Michael Roseman
Photo Editor Caroline Smith
Research Editor Danny Freedman

LIFE Magazine
Managing Editor Bill Shapiro
Creative Director Richard Baker
Executive Editorial Manager Maura Fritz
Director of Photography George Pitts

LIFE Books
President Andrew Blau
Business Manager Roger Adler
Business Development Manager Jeff Burak
Business Analyst Ka-On Lee
Editorial Director Robert Sullivan

Editorial Operations Richard K. Prue, David Sloan (DIRECTORS), Richard Shaffer (GROUP MANAGER), Burt Carnesi, Brian Fellows, Raphael Joa, Angel Mass, Stanley E. Moyse (MANAGERS), Soheila Asayesh, Keith Aurelio, Trang Ba Chuong, Ellen Bohan, Charlotte Coco, Osmar Escalona, Kevin Hart, Norma Jones, Mert Kerimoglu, Rosalie Khan, Marco Lau, Po Fung Ng, Rudi Papiri, Barry Pribula, Carina A. Rosario, Albert Rufino, Christopher Scala, Vaune Trachtman, Paul Tupay, Lionel Vargas, David Weiner

Produced By

President Julie Merberg
Editor and Photo Research Sarah Parvis

Special thanks to Patty Brown, Sara Newberry, Kate Gibson, Brian Michael Thomas, Ryan Feerer, Christine Capelli

Puzzle Photo Manipulation Reddish-Blue Inc.

Time Inc. Home Entertainment
Publisher Richard Fraiman
Executive Director, Marketing Services Carol Pittard
Director, Retail & Special Sales Tom Mifsud
Marketing Director, Branded Businesses Swati Rao
Director, New Product Development Peter Harper
Financial Director Steven Sandonato
Book Production Manager Jonathan Polsky
Marketing Manager Laura Adam
Manager, Prepress & Design Anne-Michelle Gallero

Special thanks to Bozena Bannett, Alexandra Bliss, Glenn Buonocore, Suzanne Janso, Robert Marasco, Brooke McGuire, Chavaughn Raines, Mary Sarro-Waite, Ilene Schreider, Adriana Tierno

---

PUBLISHED BY
LIFE BOOKS
Vol. 7, No. 2 • April 2007

If you would like to order any of our hardcover Collector's Edition books, please call us at 800-327-6388. (Monday through Friday, 7 a.m. to 8 p.m., or Saturday, 7 a.m. to 6 p.m. Central Time).
Please visit us, and sample past editions of LIFE, at *www.LIFE.com.*

READY, SET,

CONTENTS

NOVI

These puzzles are for everyone:
rookies and veterans,
young and old. Start here, and
sharpen your skills.

Happy Days Are Here Again

Grab an extra straw, and get going!

NOVICE

A B C D E

1 2 3 4 5

8 changes

KEEP SCORE

❑
❑
❑
❑
❑
❑
❑
❑

2min **50**sec

Answers on page 166

What's Yellow and White and Red All Over?

These trinkets just won't stay put.
How many have been tampered with?

9 changes

KEEP SCORE

❑
❑
❑
❑
❑
❑
❑
❑
❑

3min 25sec

Answers on page 166

NOVICE

Life's a Picnic . . .

. . . but this puzzle isn't. Better think outside the basket.

9
changes

KEEP SCORE

❑
❑
❑
❑
❑
❑
❑
❑
❑

A B C D E

1 2 3 4 5

3min 20sec

Answers
on page 166

AGE FOTOSTOCK/SUPERSTOCK

Even a Baby Can Do It!

Finding the changes in these pictures should be child's play

NOVICE

7 changes

KEEP SCORE

❑
❑
❑
❑
❑
❑
❑

2min 30sec

Answers on page 166

Domestic Goddess

Who says the fun has to stop when the housework begins?
You'll clean up this puzzle in no time.

NOVICE

10 changes

KEEP SCORE

❑
❑
❑
❑
❑
❑
❑
❑
❑
❑

2min 50sec

Answers on page 166

NOVICE

Something New Under the Sun

Is it a mirage, or are things moving around on this beach?

A B C D E

1 2 3 4 5

8 changes

KEEP SCORE

❑ ❑ ❑ ❑ ❑ ❑ ❑ ❑

2min 30sec

Answers on page 166

ANGELO CAVALLI/SUPERSTOCK

Make a Wish!

This puzzle can't hold a candle to your sharp eyes

A B C D E

1 2 3 4 5

10 changes

KEEP SCORE

❑ ❑ ❑ ❑ ❑ ❑ ❑ ❑ ❑ ❑

3min 15sec

Answers on page 166

NOVICE

Read Between the Lines

Don't just stand there—get to work. The clock's ticking, and these pictures are chock-full of differences.

NOVICE

A B C D E

1 2 3 4 5

10 changes

KEEP SCORE

❑ ❑ ❑ ❑ ❑ ❑ ❑ ❑ ❑ ❑

4min 15sec

Answers on page 166

Bear Necessities

This camping trio may have to make do without some essentials.
Hope it doesn't rain!

NOVICE

10
changes

KEEP SCORE

4min 5sec

Answers
on page 166

NOVICE

It's a Bird, It's a Plane, It's Superbaby!

We sliced up this photo and scrambled the pieces.
Use the boxes below to get it back in balance.

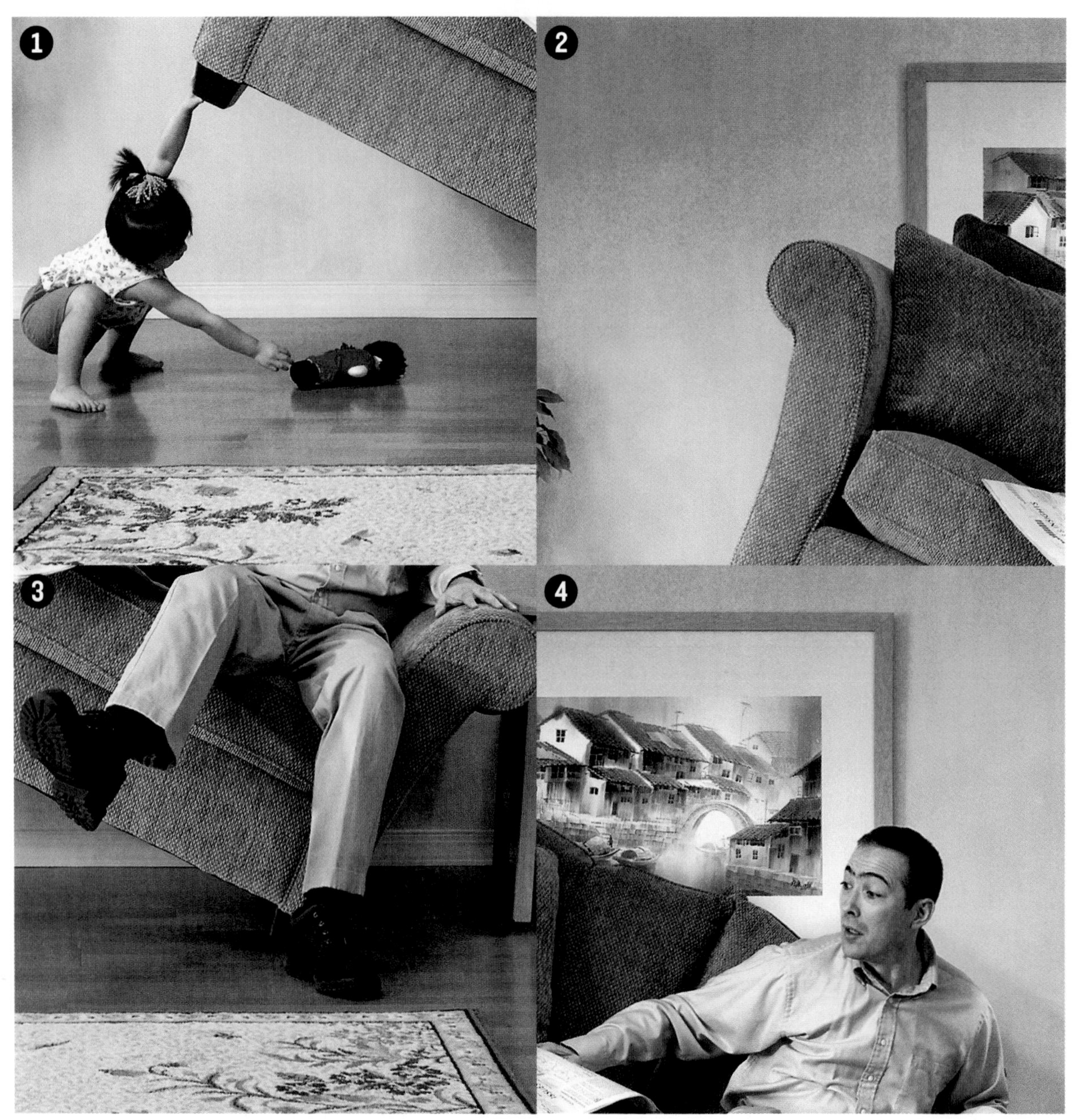

AGE FOTOSTOCK/SUPERSTOCK

0min 30sec

Answer
on page 167

KEEP SCORE

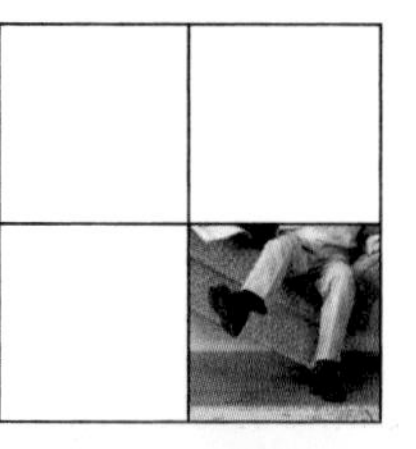

Penguins on Parade

Can you unmuddle this huddle? The grid will help those befuddled.

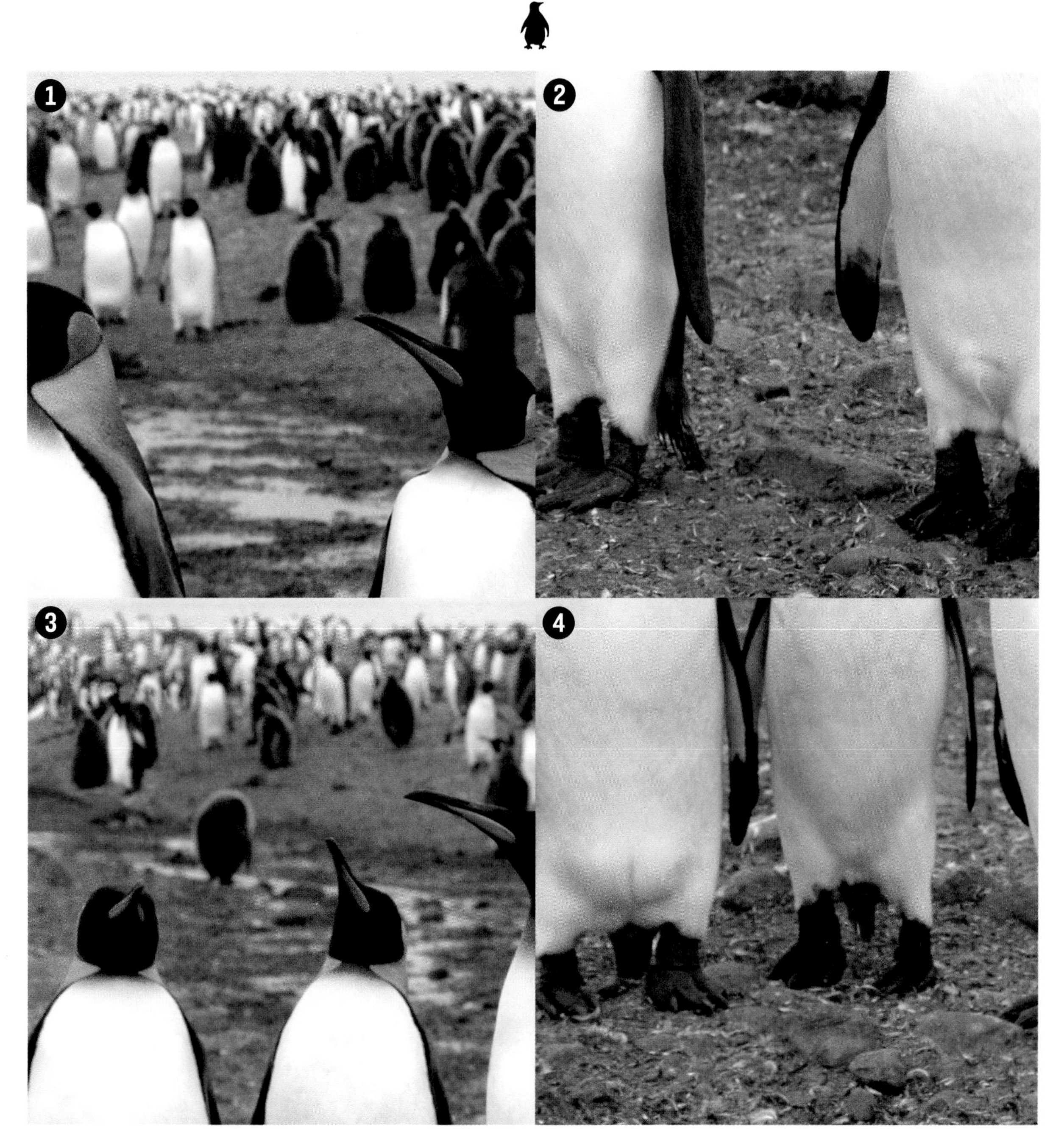

KEEP SCORE

0min 40sec

Answer on page 167

Lickety-split

A few things are amiss with these little misses. Wouldn't it be sweet if you could spot them all?

A
B
C
D
E

1 2 3 4 5

11 changes

KEEP SCORE

❑
❑
❑
❑
❑
❑
❑
❑
❑
❑
❑

3min 50sec

Answers on page 167

NOVICE

Let There Be Lights

Five of these snowmen are identical, and one is unique.
Can you tell which is warmer than the rest?

1

2

3

4

5

6

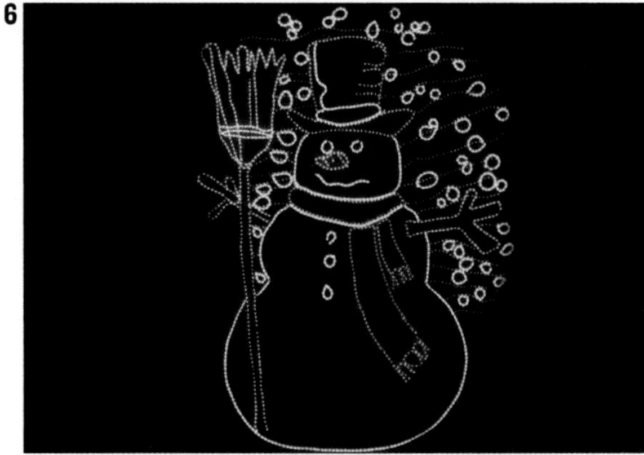

AGF FOTOSTOCK/SUPERSTOCK

0min 30sec

Answer
on page 167

That Darn Cat!

This frisky feline is up to no good.
Which of these pictures is also out of line?

1

2

3

4

5

6

0min 35sec

Answer
on page 167

Dorm-Room Disaster

The college student isn't the only thing moving in this picture.
Study hard, or it will be curtains for you.

Answers on page 167

NOVICE

AGF FOTOSTOCK/SUPERSTOCK

Shake Things Up

There's some new stuff on the menu here.
Take a seat, and start searching.

A B C D E

1 2 3 4 5

9 changes

KEEP SCORE

❑
❑
❑
❑
❑
❑
❑
❑
❑

4min 50sec

Answers on page 167

NOVICE

Quit Clowning Around

Solving this puzzle should put a smile on your face

NOVICE

11 changes

KEEP SCORE

❑
❑
❑
❑
❑
❑
❑
❑
❑
❑
❑

4min 45sec

Answers on page 167

Different Strokes

Watch out for the changing brushwork in these masterpieces

NOVICE

11 changes

KEEP SCORE

4min 30sec

Answers on page 167

Tool Time

Just because there's a wrench in the works doesn't mean you can't hammer out the solution to this puzzle

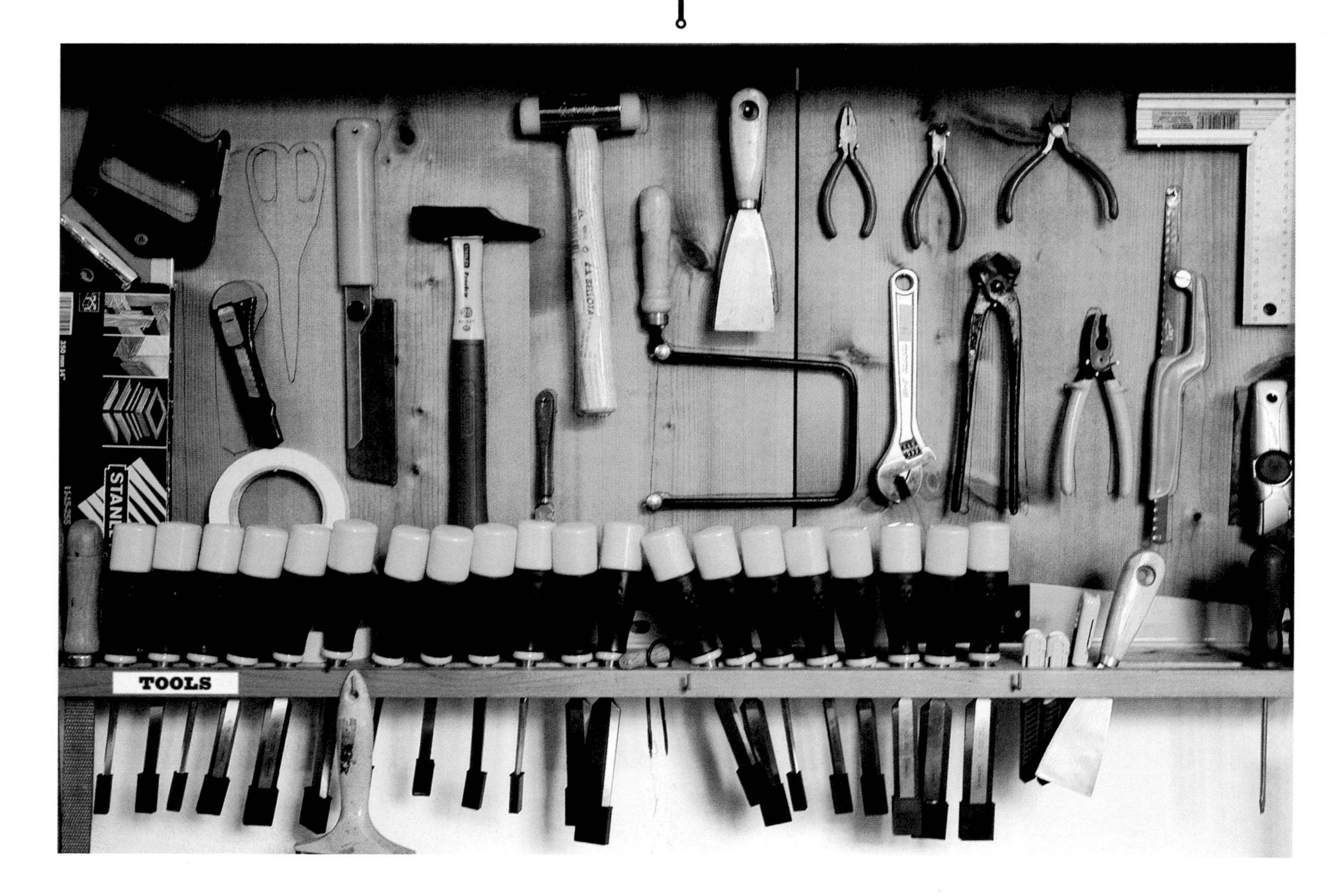

NOVICE

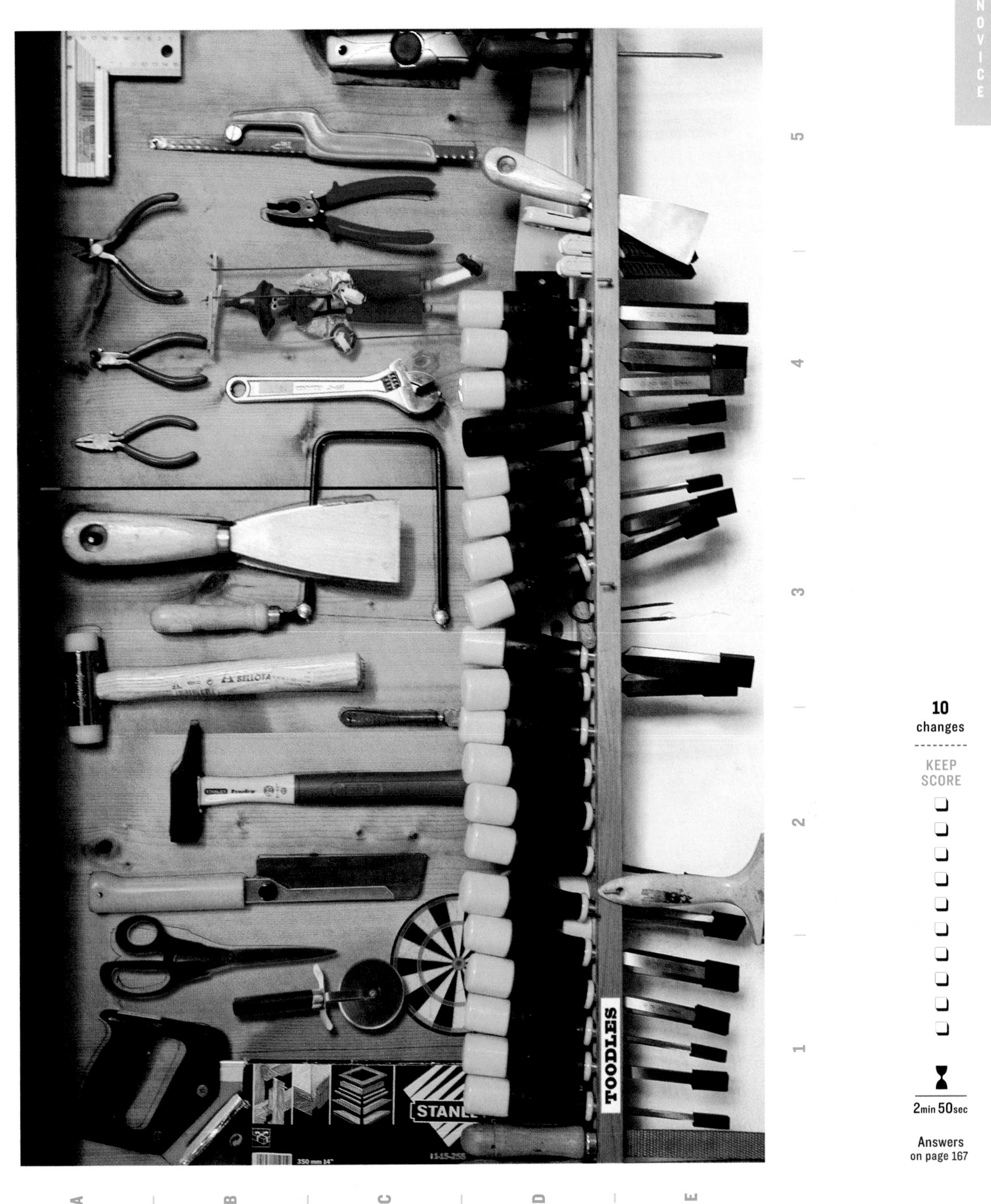

5
4
3
2
1

A
B
C
D
E

10 changes

KEEP SCORE

❑
❑
❑
❑
❑
❑
❑
❑
❑
❑

2min 50sec

Answers on page 167

NOVICE

Tickled Pink

Can you put the spring back in this girl's step?

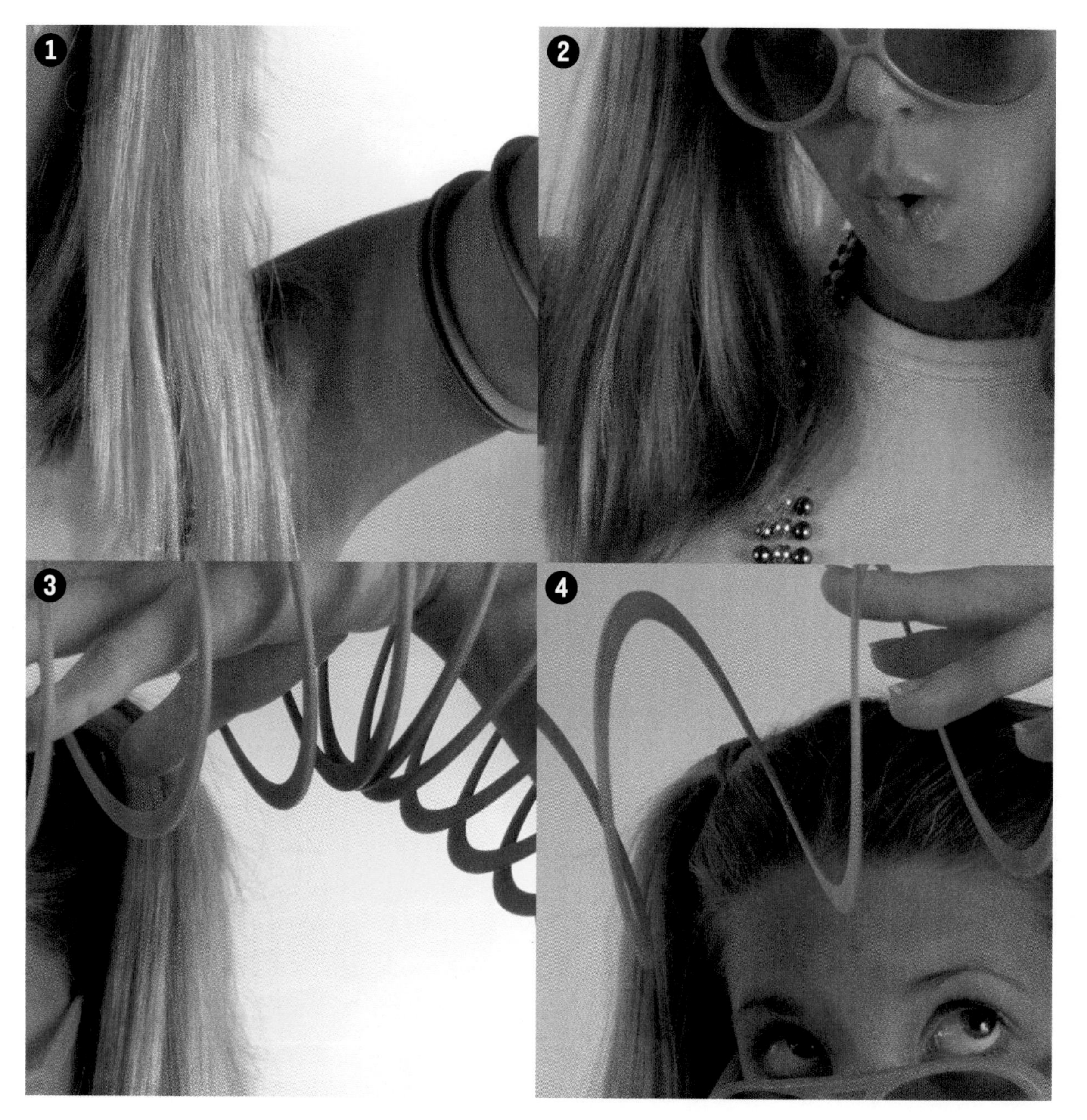

AGE FOTOSTOCK/SUPERSTOCK

0min 30sec

Answer on page 167

KEEP SCORE

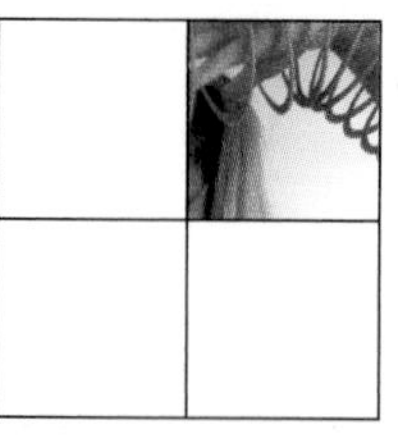

All Wrapped Up

Some packages got scrambled in transit—see if you can sort them out

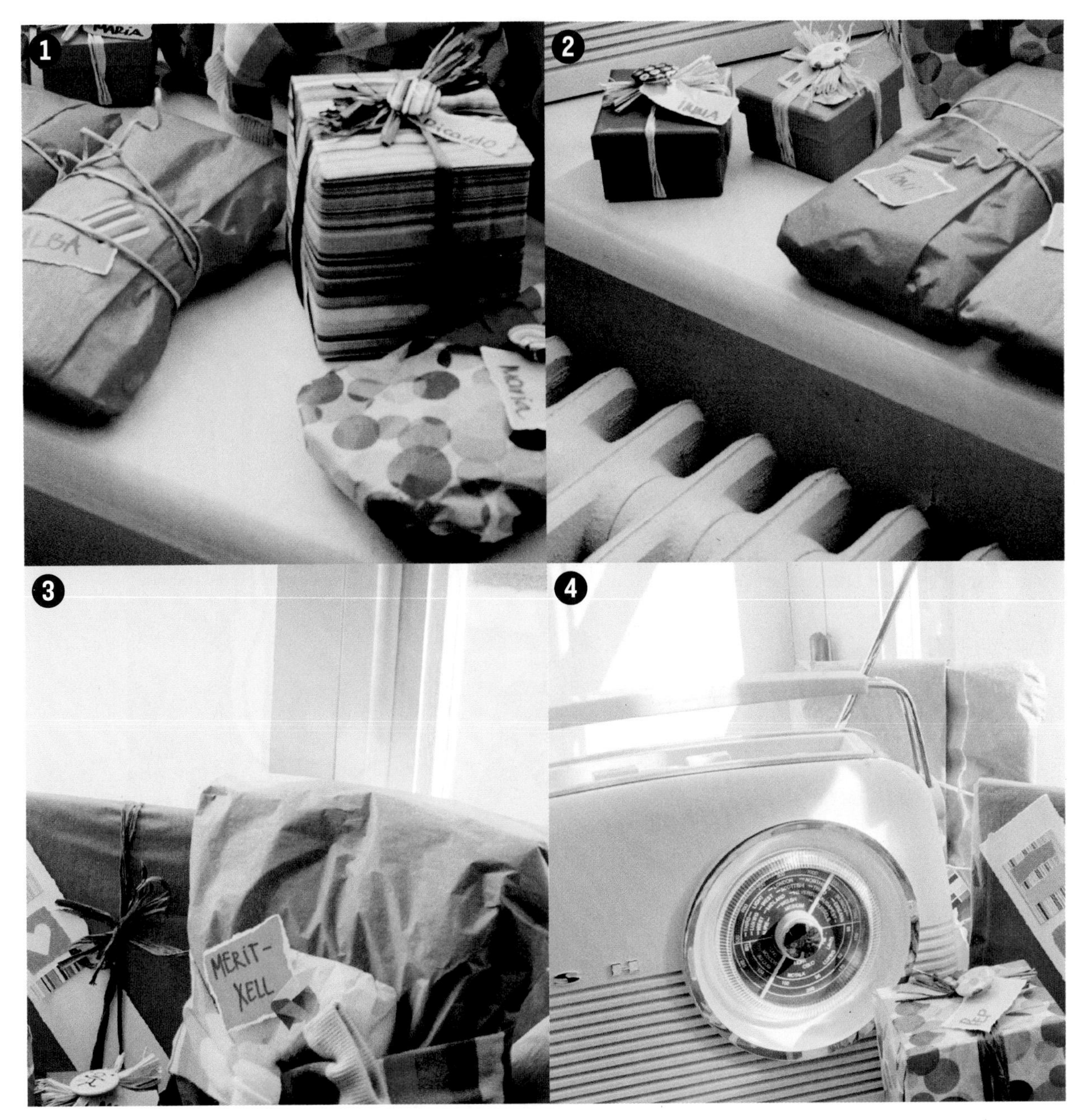

KEEP SCORE

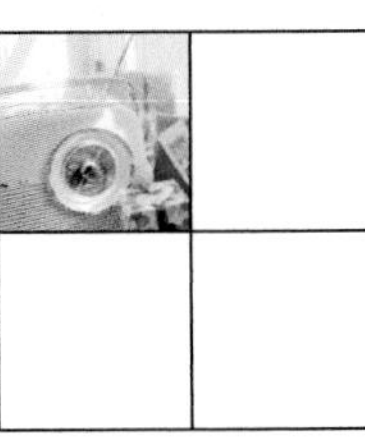

0min 45sec

Answer on page 168

NOVICE

Get Your Kicks on Route 66

You don't need to be a cowboy to round up this puzzle's altered states

NOVICE

A

B

C

D

E

1 | 2 | 3 | 4 | 5

11 changes

KEEP SCORE

- ❑
- ❑
- ❑
- ❑
- ❑
- ❑
- ❑
- ❑
- ❑
- ❑
- ❑

5min 10sec

Answers on page 168

Eighth Wonder of the World

The pyramids haven't changed much recently, but this photo sure has. Try to finish it before the full moon.

NOVICE

8
changes

KEEP SCORE

- ❑
- ❑
- ❑
- ❑
- ❑
- ❑
- ❑
- ❑

4min **10**sec

Answers
on page 168

NOVICE

Oompah-pah!

If you solve this one, go ahead and blow your own horn

A B C D E

1 2 3 4 5

10 changes

KEEP SCORE

❑ ❑ ❑ ❑ ❑ ❑ ❑ ❑ ❑ ❑

4min 50sec

Answers on page 168

STEVE VIDLER/SUPERSTOCK

Send In the Clowns

One, two, three . . . go!

NOVICE

A
B
C
D
E

1 2 3 4 5

7 changes

KEEP SCORE

❑
❑
❑
❑
❑
❑
❑

2min 45sec

Answers on page 168

NOVICE

Welcome to the Neighborhood

Try to find all the renovations to their new home

8 changes

KEEP SCORE

❑
❑
❑
❑
❑
❑
❑
❑

3min 15sec

Answers on page 168

Cloudy With a Chance of Snowman

Can you spot this homework assignment's additions and subtractions?

NOVICE

A B C D E

1 2 3 4 5

9 changes

KEEP SCORE

❑
❑
❑
❑
❑
❑
❑
❑
❑

3min 40sec

Answers on page 168

Be a Good Sport

Feel free to knock this one out of the yard

NOVICE

A

B

C

D

E

1 2 3 4 5

11 changes

KEEP SCORE

4min 30sec

Answers on page 168

DENNIS YANKUS/SUPERSTOCK

It's Not a Senior Moment

Since wisdom comes with age, these gentlemen have already solved the puzzle. Can you, Junior?

16
changes

KEEP SCORE

- [ ]
- [ ]
- [ ]
- [ ]
- [ ]
- [ ]
- [ ]
- [ ]
- [ ]
- [ ]
- [ ]
- [ ]
- [ ]
- [ ]
- [ ]
- [ ]

6min 0sec

Answers on page 168

MAST

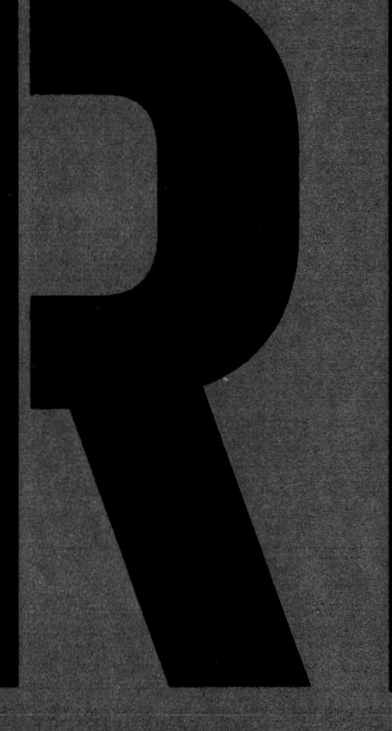

Here, puzzles get a little harder. You'll need to raise your game a level.

Plenty of Fish in the Sea

Can you reel in all eight sneaky changes at this reef?

A – B – C – D – E

1 | 2 | 3 | 4 | 5

8 changes

KEEP SCORE

❑ ❑ ❑ ❑ ❑ ❑ ❑ ❑

3min 50sec

Answers on page 169

Some Bunny Better Explain . . .

. . . what's going on in this nursery

MASTER

A — B — C — D — E

1 | 2 | 3 | 4 | 5

9 changes

KEEP SCORE

☐ ☐ ☐ ☐ ☐ ☐ ☐ ☐ ☐

4min 0sec

Answers on page 169

Don’t Be Spooked

This Halloween puzzle’s not as scary as it looks

MASTER

11
changes

KEEP SCORE

❑
❑
❑
❑
❑
❑
❑
❑
❑
❑
❑

5min 20sec

Answers on page 169

Beat the Clock

One of the few things that hasn't changed here is the time itself—but what has?

MASTER

A B C D E

1 2 3 4 5

10 changes

KEEP SCORE

3min 35sec

Answers on page 169

MASTER

What Goes Up . . .

. . . must come down. Five sets of balloons are the same, and one is full of hot air. Find it.

1

2

3

4

5

6

1min 40sec

Answer on page 169

The Answer Is Blowin' in the Wind

One of these tropical locales is unique.
So which has gone fishing?

MASTER

1

2

3

4

5

6

1min 0sec

Answer
on page 169

What’s Cookin’, Good-lookin’?

You’ll need a sharp eye to cut through the culinary confusion in these photos

M
A
S
T
E
R

12
changes

KEEP
SCORE

❑
❑
❑
❑
❑
❑
❑
❑
❑
❑
❑
❑

5min 55sec

Answers
on page 169

MASTER

Shell Game

Put a little mussel into this one

7 changes

KEEP SCORE

☐
☐
☐
☐
☐
☐
☐

4min 5sec

Answers on page 169

AGF FOTOSTOCK/SUPERSTOCK

Terminal Boredom

Why sit around? Solve this puzzle instead.

MASTER

A – B – C – D – E

1 | 2 | 3 | 4 | 5

7 changes

KEEP SCORE

❑
❑
❑
❑
❑
❑
❑

4min 55sec

Answers on page 169

Office-Supply Shake-up

Study this desk drawer carefully, and you'll soon pin down the differences

MASTER

9 changes

KEEP SCORE

❑
❑
❑
❑
❑
❑
❑
❑
❑

3min 55sec

Answers on page 169

Neighborhood Watch

Make a sweep of this street, and see what turns up

MASTER

A

B

C

D

E

1 | 2 | 3 | 4 | 5

9 changes

KEEP SCORE

4min 30sec

Answers on page 170

MASTER

Let the Sun Shine In

Can you repair this broken window scene?
Use the grid below as your guide.

AGE FOTOSTOCK/SUPERSTOCK

1min 15sec

Answer on page 170

KEEP SCORE

Postcards From the Edge

We took this tourist snapshot and mixed it up.
The burden's on you to get this scene in order.

MASTER

KEEP SCORE

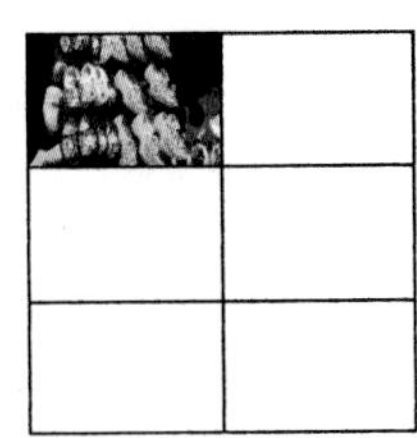

1min 35sec

Answer on page 170

Eat Your Veggies!

A few extra carrots might get your eyes in shape for this puzzle. But hurry, they're going fast.

10 changes

KEEP SCORE

❑
❑
❑
❑
❑
❑
❑
❑
❑
❑

3min 55sec

Answers on page 170

MASTER

Hats Off to You . . .

. . . if you can tie up this puzzle's loose ends

9 changes

KEEP SCORE

☐
☐
☐
☐
☐
☐
☐
☐
☐

4min 50sec

Answers on page 170

AGE FOTOSTOCK/SUPERSTOCK

Jam-packed

Step on the gas, and find the gaffes in this gridlock

12 changes

KEEP SCORE

❑
❑
❑
❑
❑
❑
❑
❑
❑
❑
❑
❑

5min 15sec

Answers on page 170

It Takes Two to Tango

Maybe you can shed a little light on this situation

MASTER

A B C D E

1 2 3 4 5

10 changes

KEEP SCORE

❑
❑
❑
❑
❑
❑
❑
❑
❑
❑

3min 45sec

Answers on page 170

The Sky's the Limit

When the going gets tough . . . well, you know the rest.
Hang in there—you can do it.

MASTER

A
B
C
D
E

1 | 2 | 3 | 4 | 5

11 changes

KEEP SCORE

5min 20sec

Answers on page 170

MASTER

Easy As Pie

We sliced up this photo and tossed it in the mixer.
Can you sort out the sweets?

MICHAEL RUTHERFORD/SUPERSTOCK

3min 15sec

Answer
on page 170

KEEP SCORE

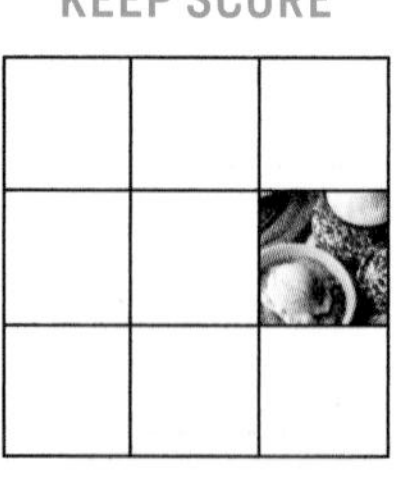

Bridal Arrangement

Something happened on the way to the wedding album.
Try to put the happy couple back together.

MASTER

KEEP SCORE

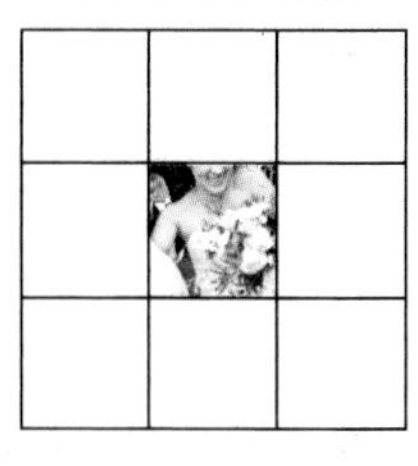

2min 20sec

Answer on page 170

Wake Up and Smell the Coffee

Someone has to monitor all the switches at this Internet café

MASTER

12 changes

KEEP SCORE

❑
❑
❑
❑
❑
❑
❑
❑
❑
❑
❑
❑

6min 30sec

Answers on page 171

MASTER

Numbers Game

The differences between these pictures will bowl you over

A – B – C – D – E

1 | 2 | 3 | 4 | 5

8 changes

KEEP SCORE

☐
☐
☐
☐
☐
☐
☐
☐

4min 30sec

Answers on page 171

AGE FOTOSTOCK/SUPERSTOCK

Paper Chase

Now, *where* did we put those eight changes?

A | B | C | D | E

1 | 2 | 3 | 4 | 5

8 changes

KEEP SCORE

❑
❑
❑
❑
❑
❑
❑
❑

3min 40sec

Answers on page 171

MASTER

Leader of the Pack

Safety first—make sure all helmets are secure and lights are on before attempting to solve this puzzle

9 changes

KEEP SCORE

7min 20sec

Answers on page 171

ALEXANDER BLACKBURN CLAYTON/PHOTOLIBRARY/PICTUREQUEST

Window Display

This intricate edifice has undergone some work. See which of its features have been remodeled.

10 changes

KEEP SCORE

❑
❑
❑
❑
❑
❑
❑
❑
❑
❑

5min 20sec

Answers on page 171

Waiting for the Other Shoe to Drop

Patterns are flip-flopping around.
Can you spot any trends among the changes?

MASTER

A
B
C
D
E
1 | 2 | 3 | 4 | 5

9 changes

KEEP SCORE

❑
❑
❑
❑
❑
❑
❑
❑
❑

4min 20sec

Answers on page 171

MASTER

Make No Bones About It

Five of these photos are the same, but one dino display is distinct. Can you uncover the beastly exhibit?

1

2

3

4

5

6

GREG MARTIN/SUPERSTOCK

1min 20sec

Answer on page 171

Life's a Beach

While all these scenes seem to match, one's actually a shade off. Which umbrellas can't stay put?

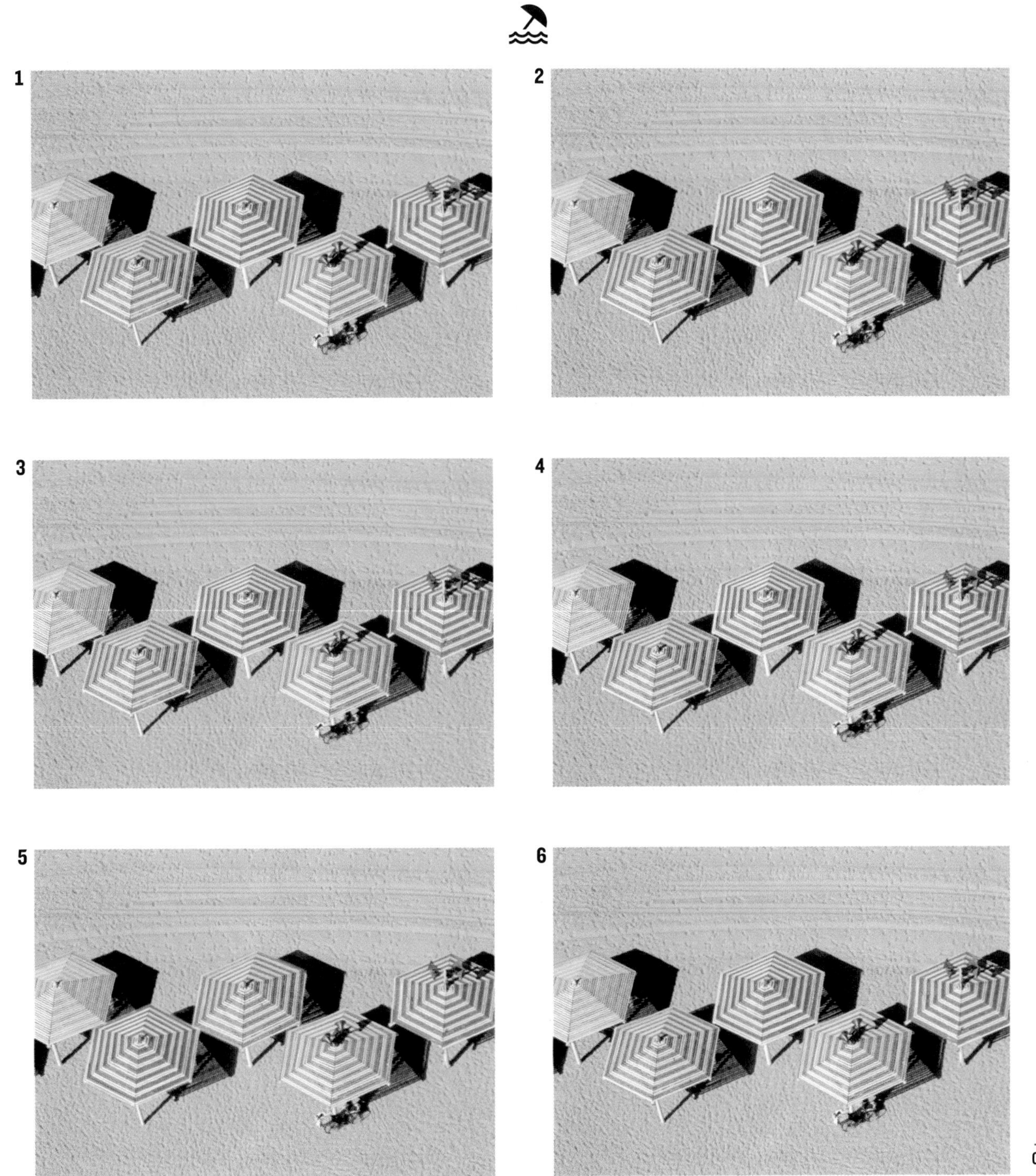

MASTER

0min 45sec

Answer on page 171

Queen for a Day

You'll have royal fun tracking down all the treasures in this well-stocked kitchen

MASTER

12
changes

KEEP SCORE

☐
☐
☐
☐
☐
☐
☐
☐
☐
☐
☐
☐

8min 40sec

Answers on page 171

Don't Shelve This One

Sorting out these sundries will have a tonic effect

MASTER

10min 20sec

Answers on page 171

EXPE

Only serious puzzlers
dare to tread past this point.
Who's in?

Seeing Spots?

It's as good a place as any to start

EXPERT

A
B
C
D
E

1 2 3 4 5

9 changes

KEEP SCORE

9min 15sec

Answers on page 172

EXPERT

No Downtime

Grab another cup of coffee. This puzzle is *not* for sleepyheads.

A B C D E

1 2 3 4 5

10 changes

KEEP SCORE

☐ ☐ ☐ ☐ ☐ ☐ ☐ ☐ ☐ ☐

9min 0sec

Answers on page 172

PETER CHIGMAROFF/SUPERSTOCK

Everything Must Go

Merchandise is really moving here—and in some cases, it's vanishing altogether

EXPERT

11 changes

KEEP SCORE

❑
❑
❑
❑
❑
❑
❑
❑
❑
❑
❑

8min 45sec

Answers on page 172

Welcome to the Dollhouse

Playtime's over. Can you face down this challenge?

EXPERT

10
changes

KEEP SCORE

☐
☐
☐
☐
☐
☐
☐
☐
☐
☐

8min 10sec

Answers on page 172

Don't Paint Yourself Into a Corner

One of these palettes is off-color.
Which is it?

1

2

3

4

5

6

3min 15sec

Answer on page 172

TERRY VINE/GETTY IMAGES

Fabric Fiesta!

A blanket is trying to pull the wool over your eyes.
Can you spot the alteration?

1

2

3

4

5

6

EXPERT

4min 15sec

Answer on page 172

Bubbling Over

We've uncorked a puzzle worth savoring.
Now *that's* reason to celebrate.

EXPERT

11 changes

KEEP SCORE

❑
❑
❑
❑
❑
❑
❑
❑
❑
❑
❑

7min 55sec

Answers on page 172

Don't Go Nuts

But do look for all the reasons these soldier photos aren't uniform

EXPERT

12
changes

KEEP SCORE

- [ ]
- [ ]
- [ ]
- [ ]
- [ ]
- [ ]
- [ ]
- [ ]
- [ ]
- [ ]
- [ ]
- [ ]

7min 40sec

Answers on page 172

Congratulations Are in Order

To you—if you locate all the items we've crashed into this wedding portrait

EXPERT

A

B

C

D

E

1 | 2 | 3 | 4 | 5

8 changes

KEEP SCORE

❑
❑
❑
❑
❑
❑
❑
❑

10min 20sec

Answers on page 172

Slightly Off-key

Mind the music stands, and you might help these symphony scenes stay in tune

EXPERT

1 2 3 4 5

A B C D E

11
changes

KEEP SCORE

❑
❑
❑
❑
❑
❑
❑
❑
❑
❑
❑

11min 25sec

Answers
on page 173

EXPERT

There Goes the Neighborhood

These houses have run amok. See if you can bring some order.

AGE FOTOSTOCK/SUPERSTOCK

6min 40sec

Answer on page 173

KEEP SCORE

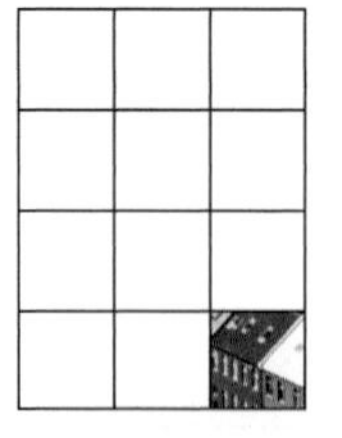

Whatever Floats Your Boat

You won't need to paddle upstream to put this patchwork right again

EXPERT

KEEP SCORE

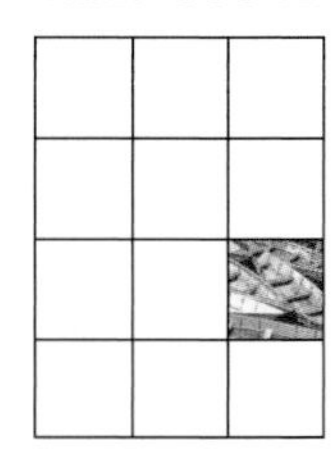

7min 25sec

Answer on page 173

Counter Intelligence

Here's the dish: These two kitchens are slightly different.
Can you spot the inconsistencies?

EXPERT

10
changes

KEEP SCORE

- [ ]
- [ ]
- [ ]
- [ ]
- [ ]
- [ ]
- [ ]
- [ ]
- [ ]
- [ ]

8min 55sec

Answers on page 173

Candy Is Dandy

Don’t let all this sugar rush to your head; unwrap our confectionary conundrum piece by piece

EXPERT

10 changes

KEEP SCORE

☐
☐
☐
☐
☐
☐
☐
☐
☐
☐

7min 15sec

Answers on page 173

Leave No Stone Unturned

A nimble-fingered sneak has made a few alterations here. Can you spot them all?

EXPERT

A B C D E

1 2 3 4 5

10 changes

KEEP SCORE

❑
❑
❑
❑
❑
❑
❑
❑
❑
❑

9min 0sec

Answers on page 173

Caught Red-handed

This puzzle's so tricky, it's practically a work of art

A B C D E

1 2 3 4 5

10 changes

KEEP SCORE

☐ ☐ ☐ ☐ ☐ ☐ ☐ ☐ ☐ ☐

7min 40sec

Answers on page 173

Make History

You don't need an advanced degree to uncover all the errors here.
An extra pencil wouldn't hurt, though.

EXPERT

A

B

C

D

E

1 | 2 | 3 | 4 | 5

12
changes

KEEP SCORE

❑
❑
❑
❑
❑
❑
❑
❑
❑
❑
❑
❑

7min **15**sec

Answers
on page 173

EXPERT

Pa-Rum-Pum-Pum-Pum

Some of these little drummers are not keeping time. Who's out of step?

A B C D E

1 2 3 4 5

AGE FOTOSTOCK/SUPERSTOCK

Dress Dilemma

It'll take a designer's eye for detail to sew this one up

EXPERT

11 changes

KEEP SCORE

☐
☐
☐
☐
☐
☐
☐
☐
☐
☐
☐

9min 40sec

Answers on page 174

Unnatural Selection

This photo has done some evolving.
Can you spot the mutations?

EXPERT

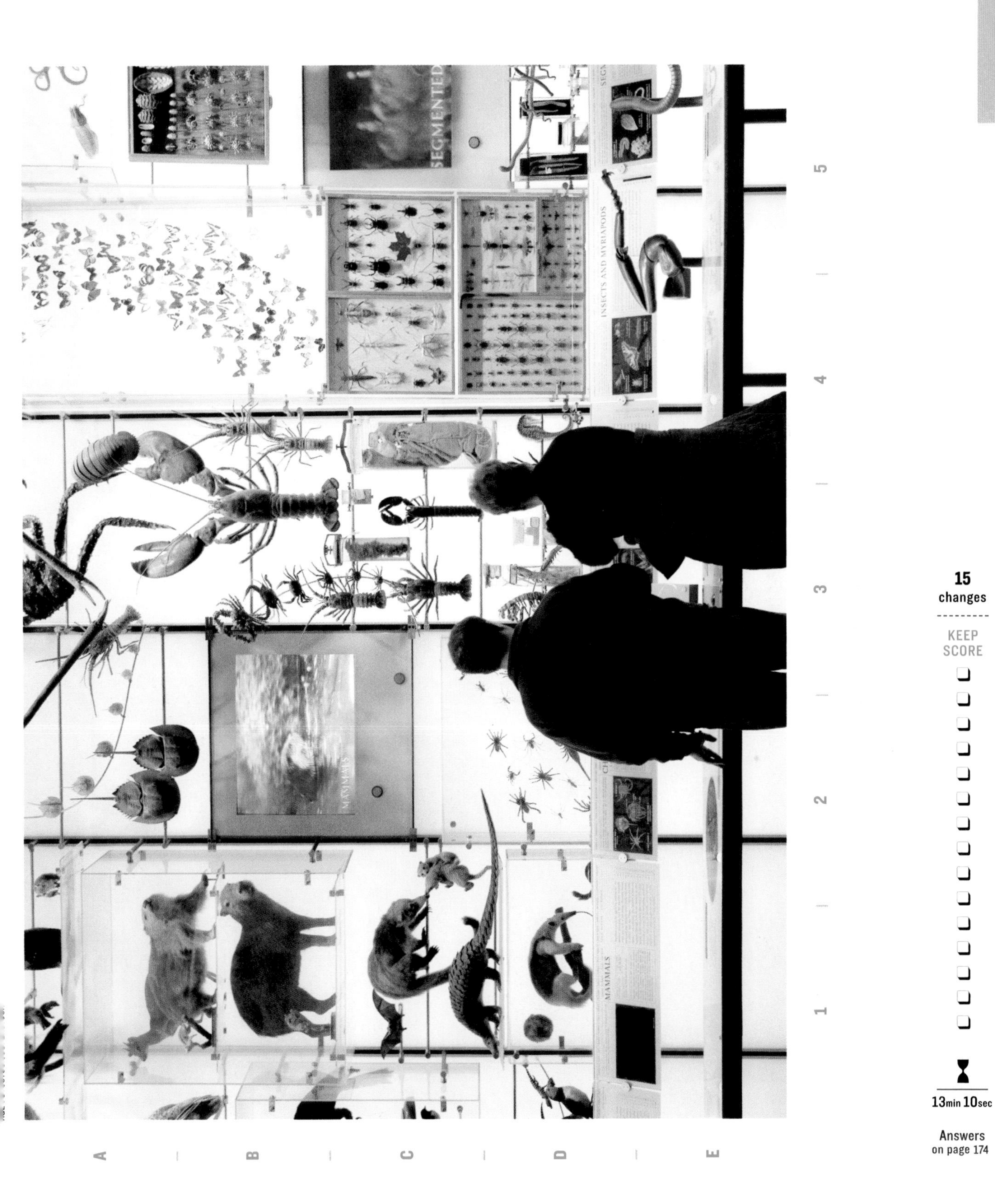

15 changes

KEEP SCORE

❑ ❑ ❑ ❑ ❑ ❑ ❑ ❑ ❑ ❑ ❑ ❑ ❑ ❑ ❑

13min 10sec

Answers on page 174

GENI

Finding a single difference in these puzzles is a challenge. Finding them all might be impossible.

Blown Out of Proportion

Talk about runaway inflation—this puzzle's packed with dastardly differences

10 changes

KEEP SCORE

☐ ☐ ☐ ☐ ☐ ☐ ☐ ☐ ☐ ☐

14min 15sec

Answers on page 174

STEVE VIDLER/SUPERSTOCK

Signs of the Times

See if you can pinpoint what's new amid the antiques in this shop

10 changes

KEEP SCORE

❑
❑
❑
❑
❑
❑
❑
❑
❑
❑

12min 30sec

Answers on page 174

JAMES L. AMOS/SUPERSTOCK

Which One Changed Its Stripes?

Examine these earrings to find the bauble that's out of line

1

2

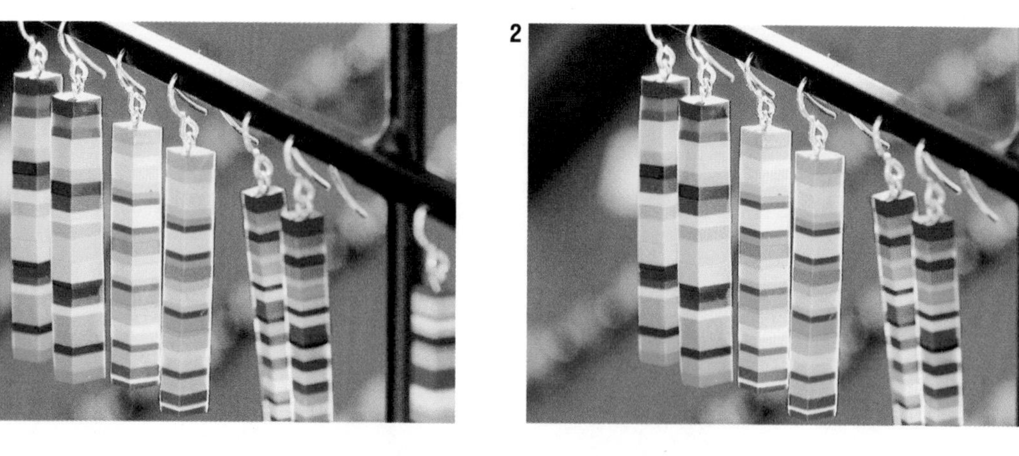

3

4

5

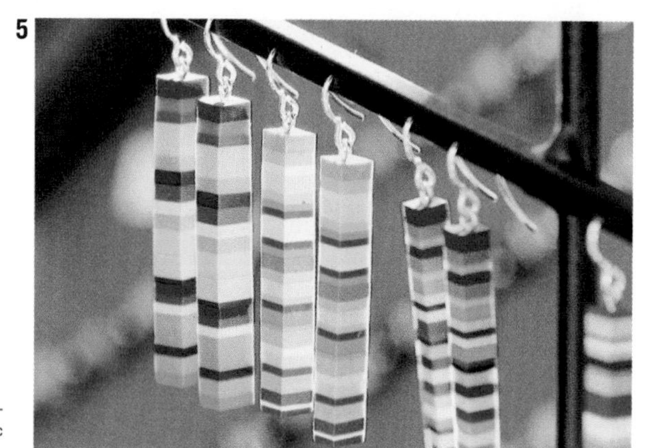

6

4min 45sec

Answer on page 174

AGE FOTOSTOCK/SUPERSTOCK

Lend Us Your Ears

Okay, we admit it: This one is next to impossible. It might sound corny, but solve it, and you're a genius.

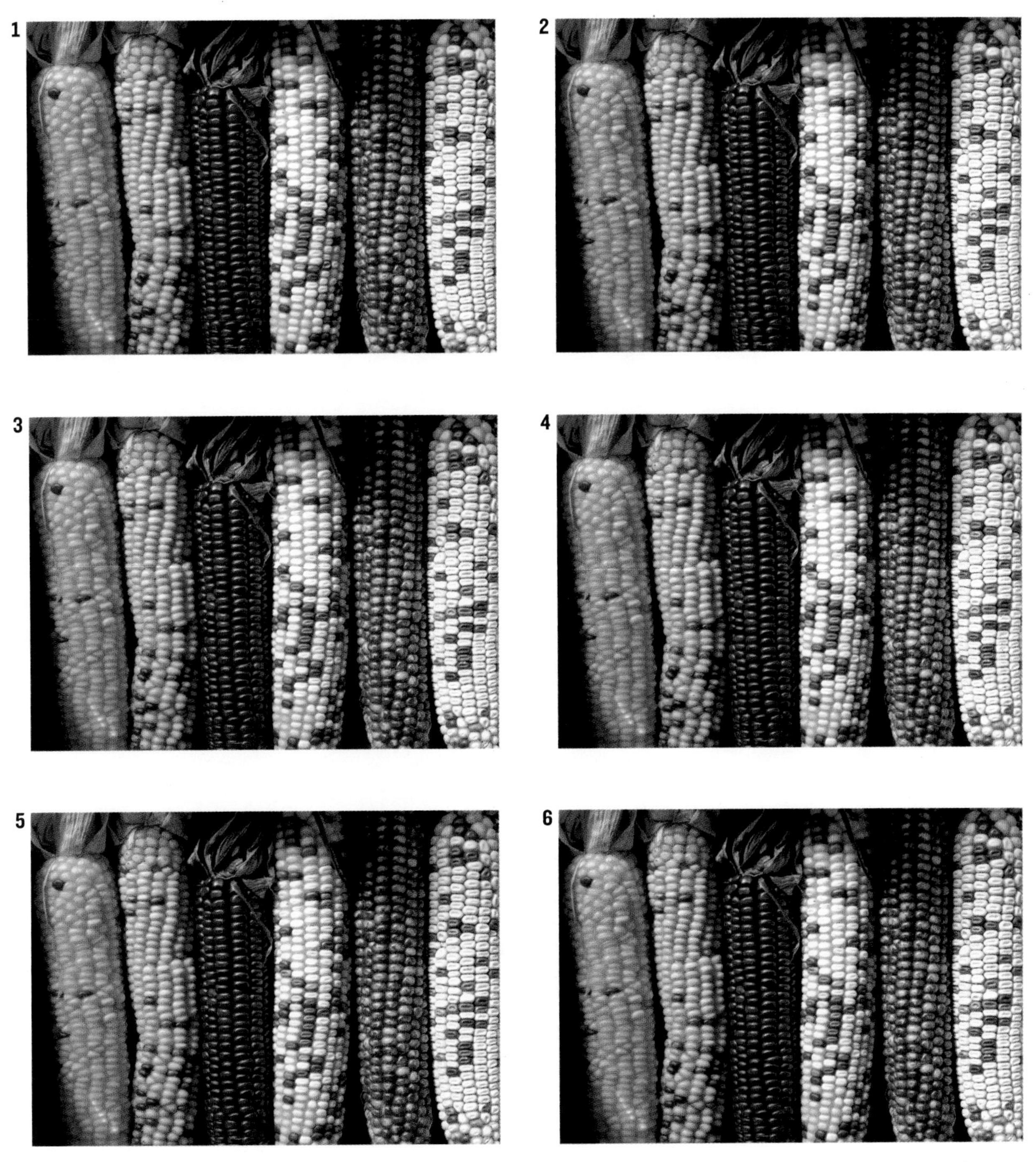

AGE FOTOSTOCK/SUPERSTOCK

8min 0sec

Answer on page 174

Housing Boom

This busy neighborhood is sure to keep you highly occupied

GENIUS

10 changes

KEEP SCORE

❑ ❑ ❑ ❑ ❑ ❑ ❑ ❑ ❑ ❑

18min 45sec

Answers on page 174

Closet Chaos

Some students didn't put their belongings away very carefully.
Can you sort things out?

A
—
B
—
C
—
D
—
E

1 | 2 | 3 | 4 | 5

10 changes

KEEP SCORE

❑
❑
❑
❑
❑
❑
❑
❑
❑
❑

13min 40sec

Answers on page 174

No Bunny Slope

Only a pro will be able to move this mountain back into place

12min 20sec

Answer
on page 174

KEEP SCORE

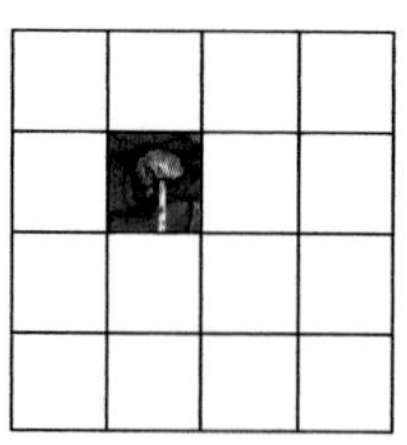

Like Mother, Like Daughter

Try to reassemble this serene scene

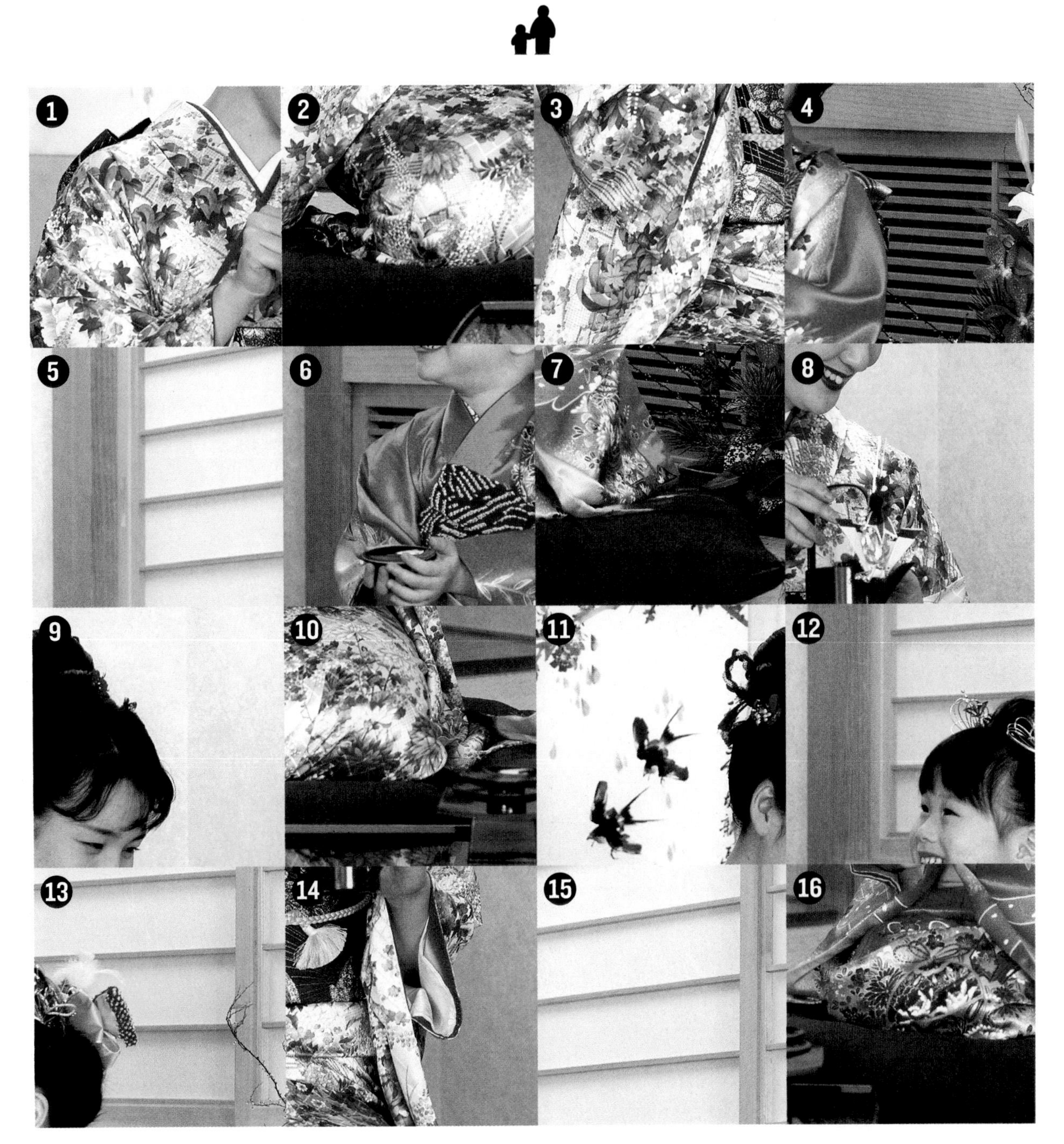

KEEP SCORE

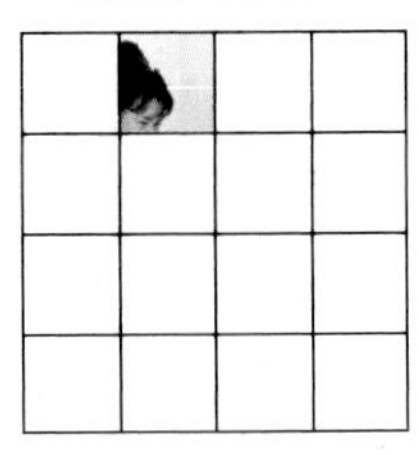

11min 15sec

Answer on page 174

Special Delivery

Avoid getting caught up in the fine print, and you'll have this one licked

1 2 3 4 5

A B C D E

COSMO CONDINA/STOCK CONNECTION/PICTUREQUEST

13 changes

KEEP SCORE

☐ ☐ ☐ ☐ ☐ ☐ ☐ ☐ ☐ ☐ ☐ ☐ ☐

20min 30sec

Answers on page 175

Masked Madness

These crafty creations are concealing lots of little alterations. You'll have to concentrate to reveal them all.

GENIUS

11
changes

KEEP SCORE

❑
❑
❑
❑
❑
❑
❑
❑
❑
❑
❑

17min 40sec

Answers on page 175

Where to Begin?

It would take an army—or a real genius—to find everything hidden in this clutter

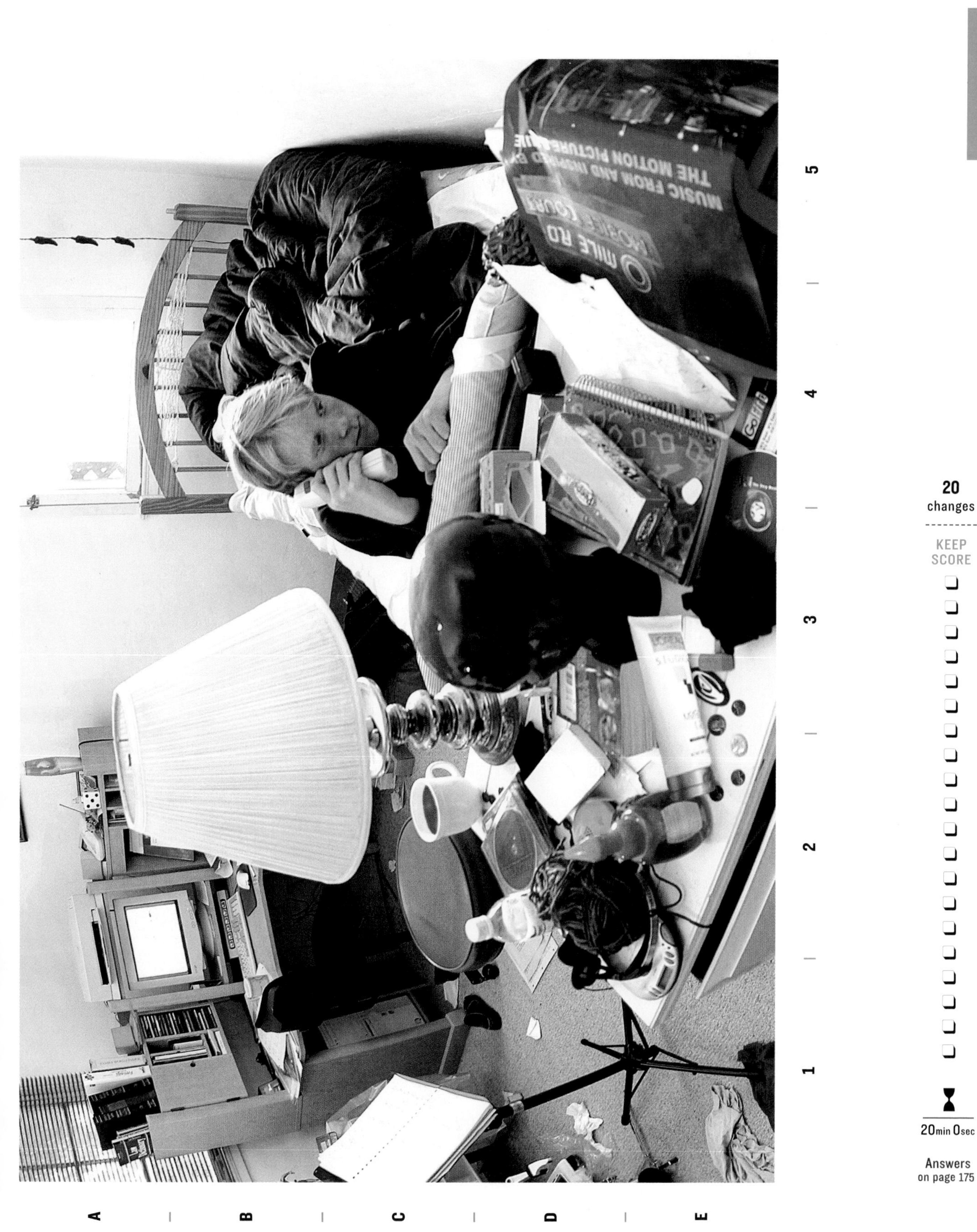

GENIUS

20 changes

KEEP SCORE

❑ ❑ ❑ ❑ ❑ ❑ ❑ ❑ ❑ ❑ ❑ ❑ ❑ ❑ ❑ ❑ ❑ ❑ ❑ ❑

20min 0sec

Answers on page 175

LIFE
CLASS

These puzzles were specially created with memorable photos from the LIFE archives.

Who Reset the Table?

This lovely food was made to order, but now it's acting disorderly.
Can you straighten it out?

9 changes

KEEP SCORE

4min 30sec

Answers on page 175

One-Stop Shopping

Keep it under your hat—this puzzle has bag-loads of surprises

A B C D E

1 2 3 4 5

11 changes

KEEP SCORE

6min 5sec

Answers on page 175

C L A S S I C S

The Man Who Has Everything

We clipped this sport into six silly pieces.
Use the chart below to make him whole again.

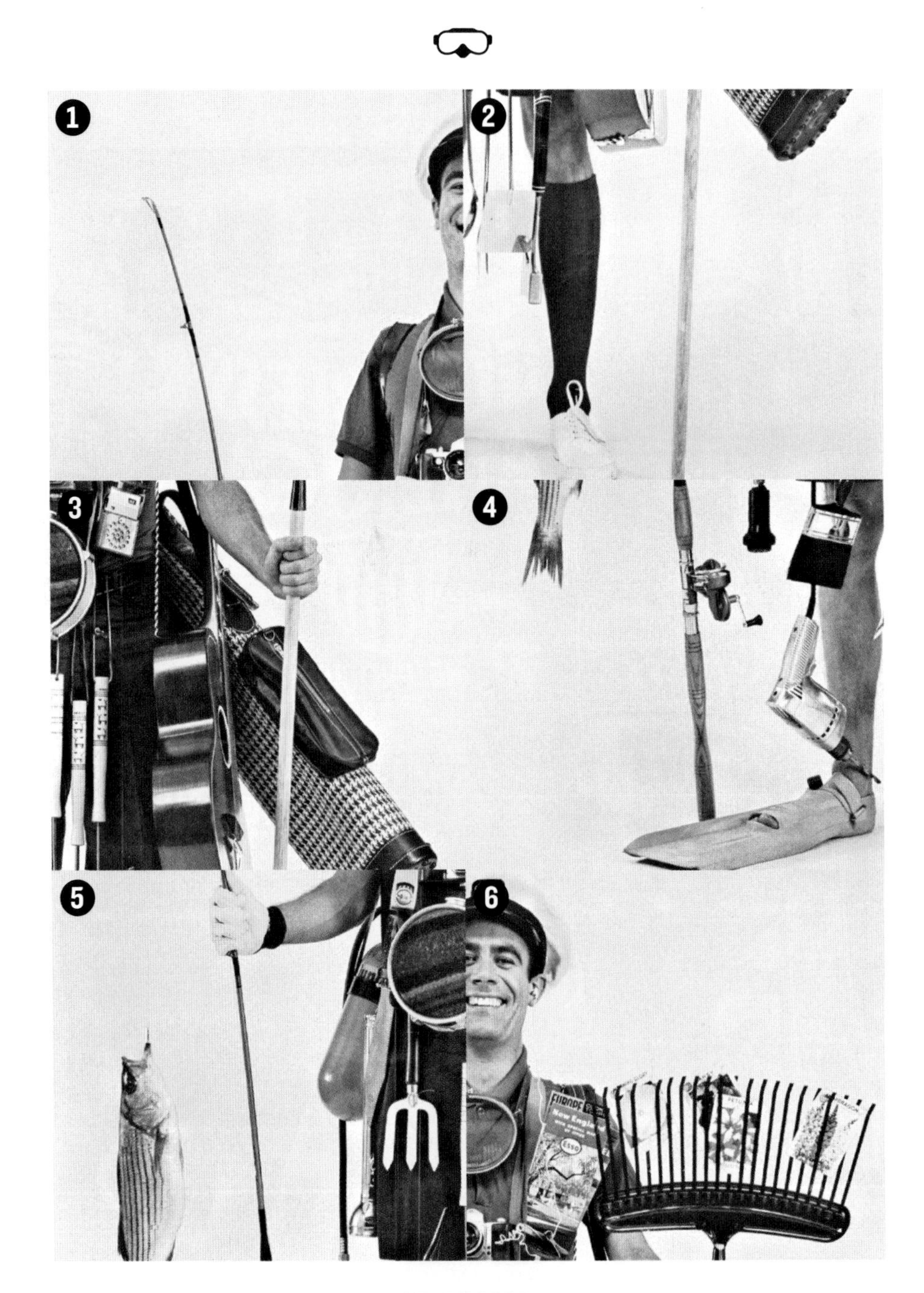

YALE JOEL/TIME LIFE PICTURES

KEEP SCORE

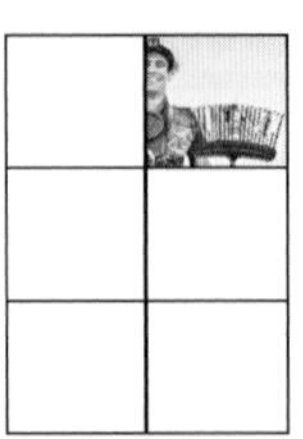

2min 20sec

Answer
on page 175

Time to Tidy Up

This furniture store has gone completely to pieces. Rearrange the rectangles to return things to normal.

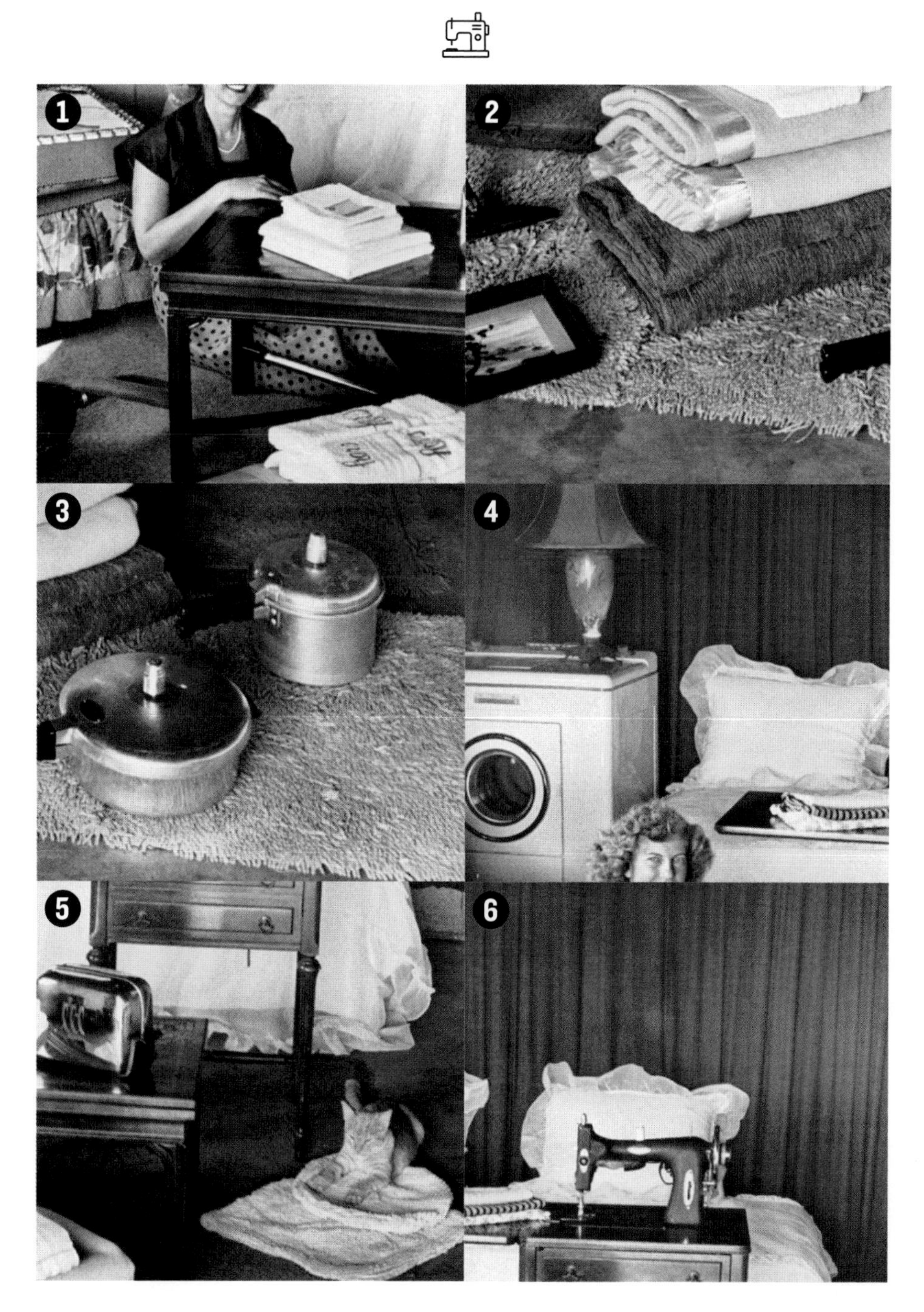

KEEP SCORE

3min 35sec

Answer on page 175

Bon Voyage

Can you unpack the differences
between these two suitcases?

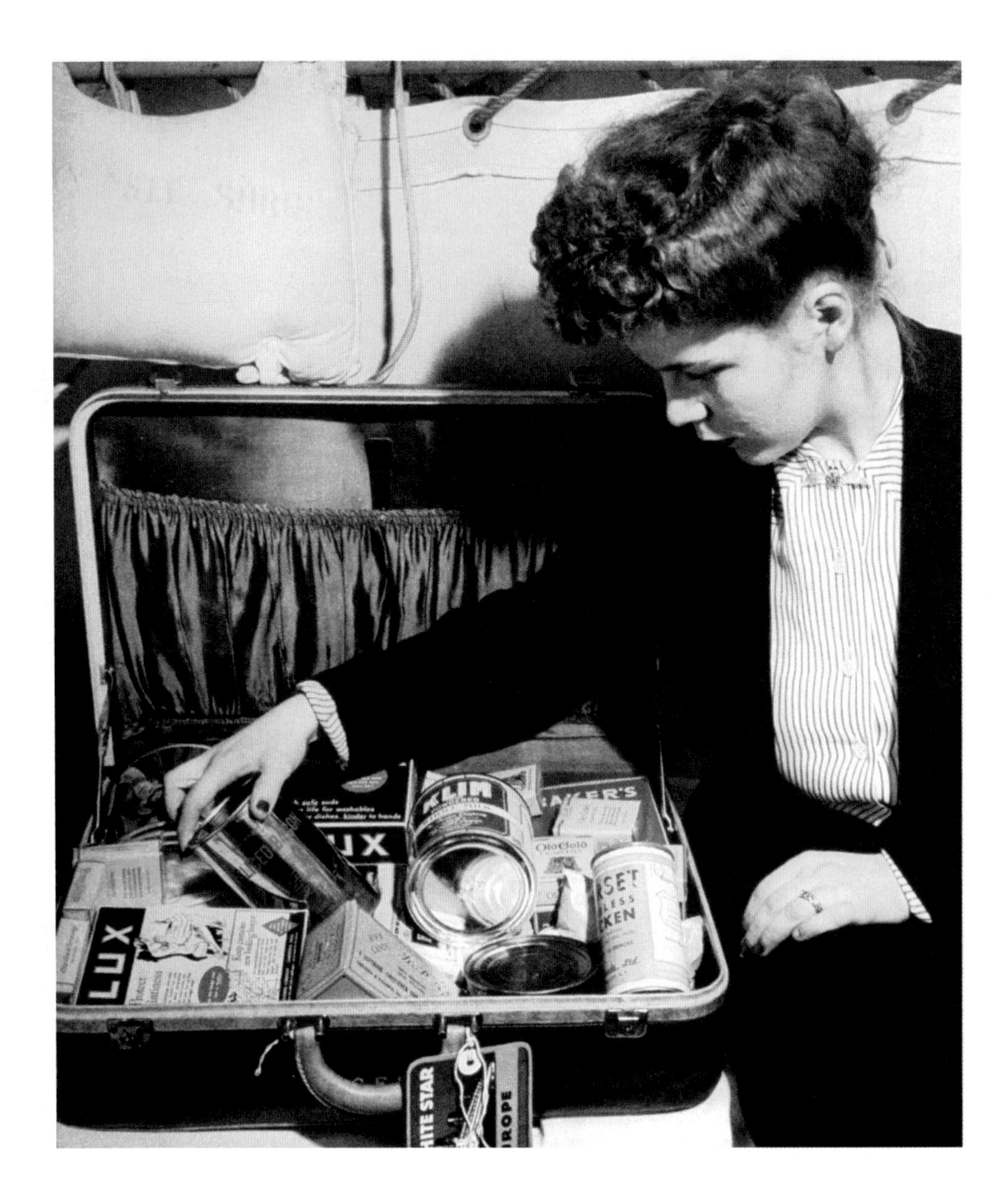

CLASSICS

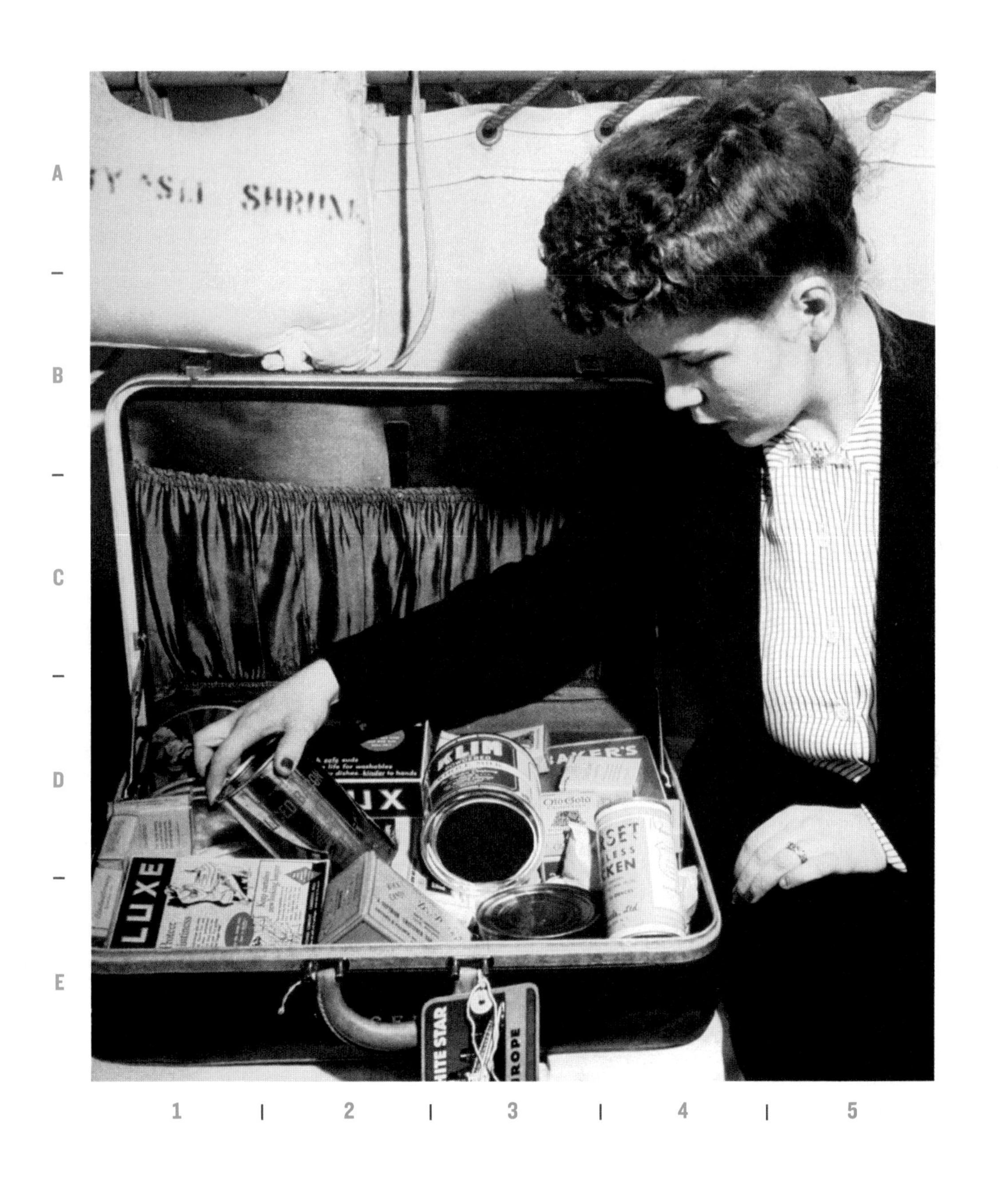

Answers on page 175

Get Back on Track

There's been a communication breakdown in the office. Help clear it up.

CLASSICS

A

B

C

D

E

1 | 2 | 3 | 4 | 5

9 changes

KEEP SCORE

❑
❑
❑
❑
❑
❑
❑
❑
❑

5min 25sec

Answers on page 176

Bumper Crop

Secrets are hiding in this garden. Better start digging.

A
B
C
D
E

1 2 3 4 5

9 changes

KEEP SCORE

❑
❑
❑
❑
❑
❑
❑
❑
❑

5min 50sec

Answers on page 176

She Couldn't Put It Down

Extra! Extra! Read all about it! Lovely lady browses modified magazines!

CLASSICS

9 changes

KEEP SCORE

❑
❑
❑
❑
❑
❑
❑
❑
❑

6min 40sec

Answers on page 176

LOOMIS DEAN/TIME LIFE PICTURES

The Party's Over?

Yes, the final puzzle has arrived.
But you're cordially invited to join us next time.

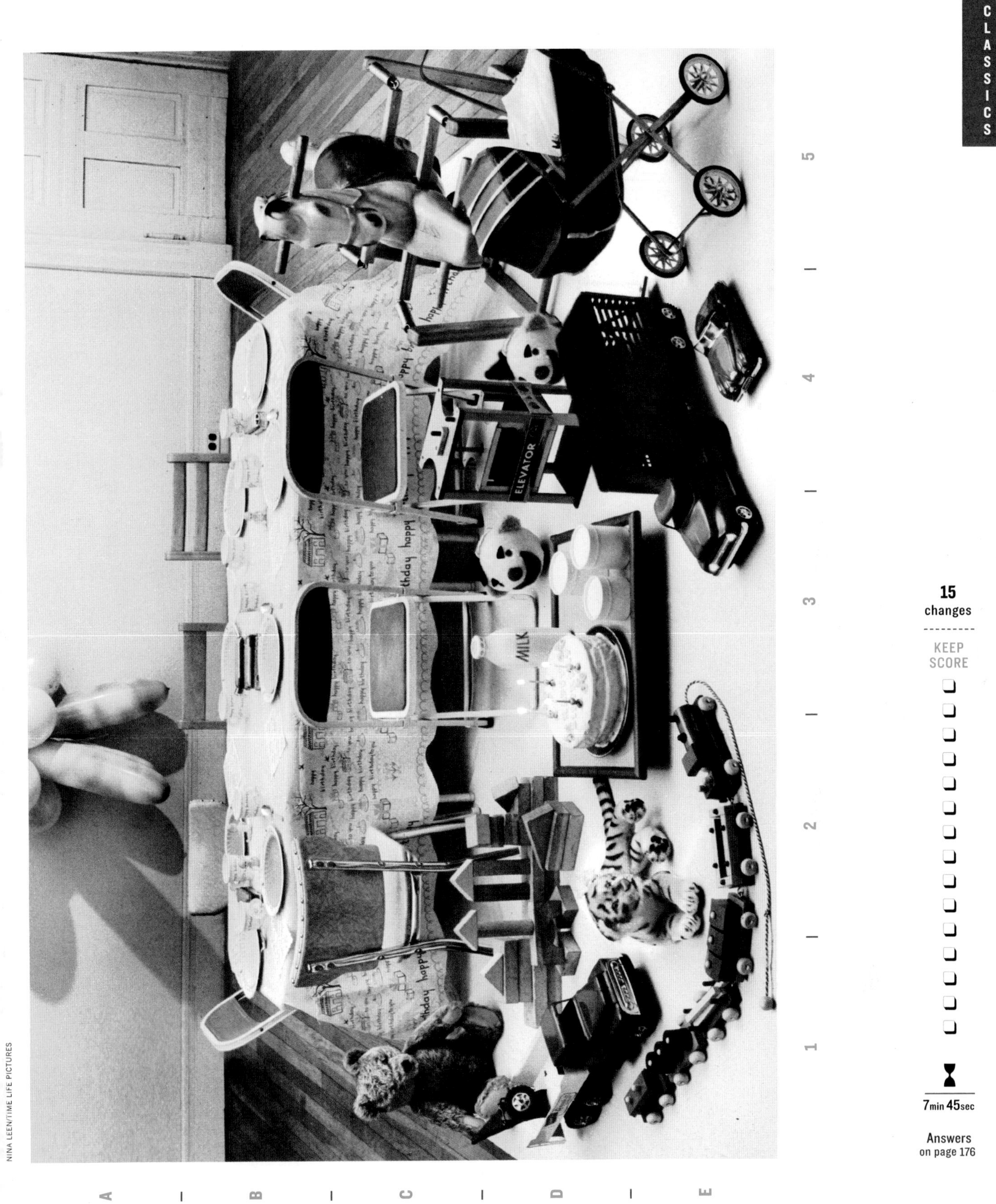

NINA LEEN/TIME LIFE PICTURES

15 changes

KEEP SCORE

☐
☐
☐
☐
☐
☐
☐
☐
☐
☐
☐
☐
☐
☐
☐

7min 45sec

Answers on page 176

[ANSWERS]

Finished already? Let's see how you did.

ANSWERS

[INTRODUCTION]

Page 3: **All Aboard!** No. 1 (B1): That's a pretty flower. No. 2 (B5 to C5): The bus grille is now completely black. No. 3 (C3): One sleeve on the boy's shirt is solid. No. 4 (C4): There is an extra panel on the bus door. No. 5 (C5): The headlight has shrunk. No. 6 (D1 to E1): A blue dot has been painted on his lunch box. No. 7 (E1): She's changed her shoes. No. 8 (E2): The red lunch bag is longer. No. 9 (E3): The blue bag has picked up two crisscrossing straps. No. 10 (E4): The WATCH YOUR STEP sign on the bus door now reads STEP YOUR WATCH.

[NOVICE]

Page 8: **Happy Days Are Here Again** No. 1 (A2): The word SODA has vanished. No. 2 (A3): ICE has become NICE. No. 3 (A4 to B4): A dime for a Coca-Cola sign? That's a fair trade. No. 4 (B3): The red sign has fallen off the wall. No. 5 (C1 to C2): The car has gotten a paint job. Classy. No. 6 (C2 to D2): Want a sip of her milk shake? Good thing there's an extra straw. No. 7 (D5): Oops—someone's lunch is on the bench. No. 8 (E2): ROUTE 66 is now ROUTE 68.

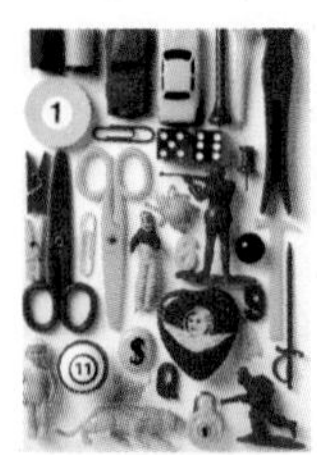

Page 10: **What's Yellow and White and Red All Over?** No. 1 (A2): The red car has turned green. No. 2 (B3 to B4): The dice have swapped spots. Places, that is. Nos. 3 and 4 (C3): Are that doll's legs shorter? And can that bee explain why? No. 5 (D1 to E2): The number 11 has been banned. No. 6 (D2 to D3): The dollar sign has morphed into an @. No. 7 (D5): The plastic number 9 is missing. No. 8 (E1): That red leotard is fetching. No. 9 (E1 to E3): The tiger has flipped.

Page 12: **Life's a Picnic . . .** No. 1 (B1): The daughter has ditched her barrettes. No. 2 (B3 to C3): Dad's shirt has lost its buttons. No. 3 (C1): Her sleeve is longer. No. 4 (C2): The beach ball's red panel has turned white. No. 5 (C4): Look, they've found a pooch! No. 6 (D2): Junior has helped himself to another sandwich. No. 7 (D3): The cooler is now labeled TEA. No. 8 (D3 to D4): The peaches have multiplied. No. 9 (E4): The hatband is gone. **Did you find the secret bonus difference? If not, log on to *www.LIFE.com* to find out what it is.**

Page 13: **Even a Baby Can Do It!** No. 1 (B5 to C5): Why the frown, Mr. Clown? No. 2 (C1): Ducky's looking awfully wide-eyed. No. 3 (C2): There is an incredible shrinking toy in the room. No. 4 (C2 to C3): Someone's been workin' on the railroad. No. 5 (C4 to D5): The laptop screen is glowing orange. No. 6 (D1): The wooden bell's blue clapper is now red. No. 7 (D1 to E1): A red flower has blossomed on the baby's back pocket.

Page 14: **Domestic Goddess** No. 1 (A1 to A2): The painting's background is now completely yellow. No. 2 (A4): Her bun is much bigger. Does that make it a loaf? No. 3 (A4 to B5): The poodle and kitty paintings have switched places. No. 4 (C1 to C2): The family portrait has been flipped upside down. No. 5 (C3): There's an extra button on the sofa back. No. 6 (C3 to C4): The hula hoop has been eighty-sixed. No. 7 (C4): She's put a jazzy new pocket on her dress. No. 8 (C4 to D5): The back of the sofa has been extended. No. 9 (E1): The vacuum now has VROOM. No. 10 (E3 to E4): She's changed her slippers.

Page 16: **Something New Under the Sun** No. 1 (A1 to B1): Oh, buoy! No. 2 (B2): Man, that water looks extra rocky today. No. 3 (B4): A white bird has perched on the rocks. No. 4 (B5): One parasol has washed away. No. 5 (C3): The center umbrella has a new pattern. No. 6 (C4): Dig those sand toys. No. 7 (D4 to D5): The yellow ring is now orange. No. 8 (E2): That umbrella is floating on air.

Page 17: **Make a Wish!** No. 1 (A2): Someone's popped the yellow balloon. No. 2 (A5 to B5): The dots on the girl's hat have lost their stripes. No. 3 (B1): What an itty-bitty hat. No. 4 (B4): That red balloon is having a great time. No. 5 (C3 to D3): A bamboo candle brings good luck. No. 6 (C4 to D4): Guess his arm got chilly. No. 7 (C5): She's had her face painted. No. 8 (D4): The boy has changed into a green shirt. No. 9 (D5 to E5): Another big present for little Johnny! No. 10 (E1 to E5): The pink trimming has fallen off the table.

Page 18: **Read Between the Lines** No. 1 (A1): Time sure has flown. At least over to this spot. No. 2 (A2 to B3): A map has replaced the artwork. No. 3 (B3): Her hat has volunteered for the Red Cross. No. 4 (B4 to C4): He's changed into a striped shirt. No. 5 (B5): Apparently the cowboy is making a formal request. No. 6 (D2): Hope she didn't need those papers. No. 7 (E2): How nice—Jimmy has signed the cast. Wait, who's Jimmy? No. 8 (E3): She's pulled up one sock. No. 9 (E4): Her shoes have turned black. No. 10 (E5): Darn litterbugs.

Page 20: **Bear Necessities** No. 1 (A4): There's an extra shoe. Must be the bear's. No. 2 (A5 to B5): The red jacket has trekked off. No. 3 (B1 to C1): Polka dots have popped up on the pillowcase. No. 4 (B2): Dad's now sporting a wristband. No. 5 (C1 to C2): Their sleeping mat has tripled in size. *Ahh.* No. 6 (C3 to D2): Dad's backpack has changed color. No. 7 (D1): A breeze has knocked over the red water bottle. No. 8 (D3): Teddy has moved his arm. Maybe he's reaching for that extra shoe. No. 9 (D5): There's pineapple for dessert. No. 10 (E5): They've upgraded to a bigger pot.

Page 22: **It's a Bird, It's a Plane, It's Superbaby!**

2	4
1	3

Page 23: **Penguins on Parade**

3	1
4	2

Page 24: **Lickety-split** No. 1 (A3): A purple butterfly has perched on her head. No. 2 (A4 to A5): Her kerchief has lost a patterned band. No. 3 (B1 to B2): Did she steal Groucho's eyebrows? No. 4 (B2): One red square has become a diamond. No. 5 (C1 to C5): The girls have swapped lollipops. No. 6 (C4): She's cut off her colorful beaded braid. No. 7 (C4 to D5): Meanwhile, she's put on a purple tank underneath her pink one. No. 8 (D5 to E5): The white heart on her top has grown. No. 9 (E1): She's removed a bracelet. No. 10 (E1 to E3): Belly shirts are out. No. 11 (E4): Ooh, who's got bling?

Page 26: **Let There Be Lights**
In photo No. 6, Frosty's scarf has gotten longer.

Page 27: **That Darn Cat!**
Someone has swiped a goldfish from photo No. 4. A suspect is in custody.

Page 28: **Dorm-Room Disaster** No. 1 (A2): He must have switched to those "green" lightbulbs. No. 2 (A2 to A5): It's curtains for you. No. 3 (B2 to B3): He's got ring around the collar (and sleeves). No. 4 (B4 to C5): There's a stack of clothes on the chair. No. 5 (D1): Okay, we get it—the stuff in the box is *fragile*. Nos. 6 and 7 (D2): He's stacked some more CDs on the pile and plunked some flowers in the vase. Just making himself at home. No. 8 (D4): The guitar strings are shorter. No. 9 (E3): His shoelace is yellow. No. 10 (E4): The soccer ball has lost a patch.

Page 29: **Shake Things Up** No. 1 (A3): The shelf is bright red. No. 2 (A5): One giant strawberry has escaped death by milk shake. No. 3 (C1): Was her skirt too short? No. 4 (C2): She's slipped on a bracelet. No. 5 (C3): Now serving chocolate milk! No. 6 (C4 to D4): The mixer has gained a third ridge. No. 7 (D1): Somebody's dropped a Slinky. No. 8 (D5): Who ordered a soda? No. 9 (E2): That black trim on her uniform is dandy.

Page 30: **Quit Clowning Around** No. 1 (A1): The white button is gone. No. 2 (B1): The yellow button has turned upside down. No. 3 (B3 to B4): Someone's looking a bit green. Nos. 4 and 5 (B5): Tough day at the circus: One guy is bummed, and another has lost the whites of his eyes. No. 6 (C2 to D2): Sorry, Mr. Ant—picnic's on page 12. No. 7 (C2 to C3): That clown must have been using Rogaine. (Actually, it's a toupee. *Shh.*) Nos. 8 and 9 (D1): This fella's crazy eyebrows make him look angry. And the poor red-faced guy above him has been rendered speechless. No. 10 (D4): This clown has lost his sight. No. 11 (E4 to E5): One button sure has grown.

Page 32: **Different Strokes** No. 1 (A2): There's a paintbrush in her back pocket. No. 2 (A4 to A5): The blue artwork has moved up. No. 3 (B3 to C3): That bloom has a new look. No. 4 (C1 to C2): The flower's leaves have become fuller. No. 5 (C3 to D3): She's dressed up her hair with a few more pink bands. So arty. No. 6 (C5 to D5): He's picked up a paintbrush. No. 7 (D1 to D2): Caution! One of the ladder's support bars is missing. No. 8 (D4): More splashes of red paint are just what that wall needed. No. 9 (E1): A few brushes have been added to the bucket. No. 10 (E4): Is that his black paint? No. 11 (E5): The red lid has outgrown its jar.

Page 34: **Tool Time** No. 1 (A1 to C1): It was about time someone returned the scissors. No. 2 (A3 to C3): The scrapers have been supersized. No. 3 (B1 to C1): Box cutter, no. Pizza cutter, yes. No. 4 (B4 to C4): Bolt cutters are out. Marionettes are in. No. 5 (B5): The ruler is coming up short. No. 6 (C1 to C2): Nice dartboard. No. 7 (C5): The yellow pliers got the blues. No. 8 (D1): Say hello to TOODLES. No. 9 (D4): A black handle is so chic. No. 10 (E2): Three chisel heads have disappeared.

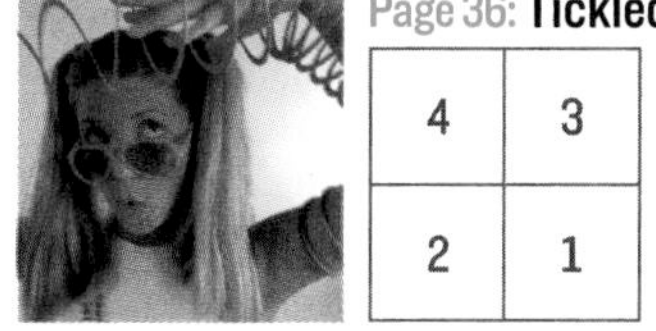

Page 36: **Tickled Pink**

4	3
2	1

Page 37: **All Wrapped Up**

4	3
2	1

Page 38: **Get Your Kicks on Route 66** No. 1 (A1): The steer horn curves at the top. No. 2 (B2): What a steal—only $5! No. 3 (B3): The boot has earned a spur. No. 4 (B4 to B5): A happy couple have etched their initials in the fence post. No. 5 (C1): The chimney has gone up in smoke. No. 6 (C2 to D2): Someone's painted the door pink. No. 7 (C4): Route 66 is now Route 99. Please note this on your map. No. 8 (D5): Contrary to popular belief, Illinois is actually the LAND OF LINCOLN *LOGS*. No. 9 (E1 to E2): This town has horns aplenty. No. 10 (E4): *LV* has been removed from the license plate. No. 11 (E5): The number 5 is backward.

Page 40: **Eighth Wonder of the World** No. 1 (A1): The moon has risen early. No. 2 (A2): Something's perked up that camel's ear. No. 3 (A5): A yellow pom-pom sits atop the camel's head. No. 4 (B4): Why is this camel smiling? No. 5 (D1 to D2): One yellow pom-pom has doubled in size. No. 6 (D4 to E5): Did a pyramid vanish, or is that a mirage? No. 7 (E1): A blue pom-pom has turned magenta. No. 8 (E4): Come on in—door's open. **Did you find the secret bonus difference? If not, log on to *www.LIFE.com* to find out what it is.**

Page 42: **Oompah-pah!** No. 1 (A1 to B5): What a beautiful blue sky. No. 2 (A2 to A3): The tuba is longer. No. 3 (B1): There's a pink feather in his cap. No. 4 (B3 to C3): He's put on a patterned shirt. Sharp. No. 5 (B4 to B5): One clever trombonist is doing Picture Puzzles while he blows his horn. No. 6 (B5): The music stand has migrated to the top of the horn. No. 7 (C1): *Mmm-mmm,* that drum sounds sweet. No. 8 (D2 to E2): One musician has a super-stripy sock. Is that regulation? No. 9 (D5): A leg of his shorts has grown longer. No. 10 (E4): Those boots were *not* made for walking.

Page 43: **Send In the Clowns** No. 1 (A1 to B1): Someone's snagged the sign from the wall. No. 2 (A1 to B2): Contestant number one is winning—the red balloon is almost full. No. 3 (A5 to B5): The 3 has become a 4. Must be this new math. No. 4 (C3): One clown has opened his eyes. No. 5 (C5): The pink hat goes so much better with his ensemble. No. 6 (D3): Not every clown could pull off a heart earring. No. 7 (D4 to E4): Who's the new guy?

Page 44: **Welcome to the Neighborhood** No. 1 (A2 to B5): The roof is a different color. No. 2 (A2): Their real estate agent threw in a new chimney. No. 3 (B1 to C1): Yes, a hanging plant definitely makes a new house a home. No. 4 (C4): Those are mighty fine buttons. No. 5 (C5): The windows have multiplied. No. 6 (D2 to D3): The stripe on his shirt has grown wider. No. 7 (D4 to E5): The garage door is open. No. 8 (E5): The letter *N* is backward.

Page 45: **Cloudy With a Chance of Snowman** No. 1 (A4 to B5): The artwork is bigger. No. 2 (B1): The electrical outlet has charged northward. No. 3 (B3 to C3): Hey, Red! No. 4 (C2 to D2): The sun's rays are longer. No. 5 (C3): She's put on lipstick. No. 6 (C5): Two prize ribbons have swapped places. No. 7 (D4): Holy cotton crafts—there's a snowman! No. 8 (E2): The ladybugs are multiplying. No. 9 (E2 to E3): The mud has dried up—and taken the pigs with it.

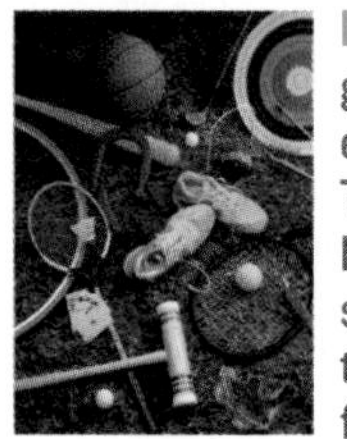

Page 46: **Be a Good Sport** No. 1 (A1): A baseball glove has joined the lineup. No. 2 (A2): Someone's erased the logo from the basketball. No. 3 (A5 to B5): The bull's-eye colors have been swapped. No. 4 (B4): The croquet ball has earned more stripes. No. 5 (C2): The tip of the shuttlecock has turned blue. No. 6 (D2): Seems diamonds *aren't* forever—the ace is now a spade. Nos. 7 and 8 (D4): Don't trip on that extra-long shoelace. And don't even think about trying to serve that billiard ball. No. 9 (D4 to D5): Wow, that racket needs restringing. No. 10 (E2): The golf ball has grown. No. 11 (E2 to E3): The badminton racket needs to get a grip.

Page 48: **It's Not a Senior Moment** No. 1 (A1 to A2): The votes are in—he's number one. No. 2 (A2): He's going to have a hard time breathing through that banana. Nos. 3 and 4 (A3): He's swapped his red visor for a blue one, and the golf club's head has gotten bigger. No. 5 (A5 to B5): Pops has caught a fish! No. 6 (B2 to C2): The snorkeler has scored some bling. No. 7 (B3): Two buttons are better than one. No. 8 (B4): A mustache suits him. No. 9 (B5 to D5): The cyclist's shirt has changed color. No. 10 (C1): That's one impressive wristband. No. 11 (C1 to E2): His pants are now red. No. 12 (C4 to D4): The handle of his fishing rod has turned yellow. No. 13 (D2): This flipper looks hipper. No. 14 (D3 to D4): With all the fish he's catching, good thing his basket has gotten bigger. No. 15 (D5): The bike's handlebar is longer. No. 16 (E2): He must have snagged his shorts and sewn on a patch.

[MASTER]

Page 52: **Plenty of Fish in the Sea**
No. 1 (A1): A scuba diver has swum onto the scene. No. 2 (A2): There's a new fish in school. No. 3 (B1): A yellow fish has turned orange. No. 4 (B5 to C5): A bunch of minnows has vanished. *Gulp.* No. 5 (C4): The patch around a yellow fish's eye is gone. No. 6 (D2 to D3): That rebel is swimming against the current. No. 7 (D5 to E5): Talk about sunken treasure—there's a castle down there! No. 8 (E3): One goldfish has wandered off.

Page 53: **Some Bunny Better Explain . . .**
No. 1 (A3): The flower on the bunny's hat is now pink in the middle. No. 2 (B5): He's no snob, but this bear's nose has been turned up. No. 3 (C4): That yellow bear sure looks happy. No. 4 (D2 to E3): Has that little bear been walking in ink? His feet are black. No. 5 (D3): It's a boy! His outfit has a blue bow now. No. 6 (D5): The brown bear's ribbon is longer. Nos. 7 and 8 (D5 to E5): The chick got toes *and* a brand-new bag. No. 9 (E2 to E3): Whoa, Ducky, chill out. **Did you find the secret bonus difference? If not, log on to *www.LIFE.com* to find out what it is.**

Page 54: **Don't Be Spooked** No. 1 (A1): Now appearing on a column: Frankenstein. No. 2 (A4 to B5): The witch's hat is extra-large. No. 3 (A5): There are more panes on the window (better for soaping!). No. 4 (B1): The boy's crown is taller. No. 5 (B4): A true princess wears a tiara. No. 6 (B4 to D5): She can trick-or-treat faster on her handy broom. No. 7 (C5): The pumpkin has been carved into a jack-o'-lantern. No. 8 (D4): This little lion has grown a tail. No. 9 (E1 to E2): Several small bricks have merged into a big one. No. 10 (E2): The pirate will be warmer on the high seas with longer pants. No. 11 (E5): More leaves have blown onto the patio.

Page 56: **Beat the Clock** No. 1 (A3): The point on top of the clock is bigger. No. 2 (B1 to C2): The figure has shrunk. No. 3 (B3): The clock will never strike three again. No. 4 (C4): The book's gold decal has worn off. No. 5 (C5 to D5): Daddy's little girl has been dumped for man's best friend. No. 6 (D2 to D3): The gold sundial paperweight has gotten weightier. No. 7 (D4 to E3): This must be a checkbook. No. 8 (E1 to E2): Is that the key to the safe? Nos. 9 and 10 (E4 to E5): The two coins at the bottom-right corner of the case have switched places, and a knot in the wood has disappeared.

Page 58: **What Goes Up . . .** In photo No. 4, a red patch has replaced a yellow one on the big balloon on the far right.

Page 59: **The Answer Is Blowin' in the Wind**
The middle boat has drifted starboard (that's to the right, for all you landlubbers) in picture No. 6.

Page 60: **What's Cookin', Good-lookin'?**
No. 1 (A2): How nice—Patty called. No. 2 (A4): That door hinge is *huge.* No. 3 (A4 to B4): Has anybody seen the exit? No. 4 (B2): The electric socket has taken off like a rocket. Nos. 5 and 6 (B5): She's removed her necklace—or did it drop in the pot?—and she's pulled up her apron. No. 7 (C1): There's a cutting-edge knife block on the counter. No. 8 (D1 to E1): Three onions have jumped into the basket. No. 9 (D2): One of the drawers has ditched a handle. No. 10 (D2 to E3): He's now slicing with measured strokes. Nos. 11 and 12 (E2): The saltshaker has slipped away. And who ate the cucumbers?

Page 62: **Shell Game** No. 1 (A3 to B3): The pattern on the conical shell has washed off. No. 2 (B1 to C2): Someone's a little crabby. No. 3 (B5): A baseball has rolled into the picture. No. 4 (C4 to D4): A tan shell has hit a growth spurt. No. 5 (D5): The brown shell has turned gray. No. 6 (E2 to E3): A new shell has appeared. No. 7 (E5): That guy looks good in stripes.

Page 63: **Terminal Boredom** No. 1 (B1 to B2): His hat has taken a turn for the silly. No. 2 (B2): She's polished off her croissant and moved on to an ice cream cone. No. 3 (B5): The crew has finished painting the column black. No. 4 (C4): His future's so bright, he needs two pairs of shades. No. 5 (D5 to E5): A chair leg has been added. No. 6 (E2): The black circle has fallen off the bag. No. 7 (E3): The shoulder strap is longer. **Did you find the secret bonus difference? If not, log on to *www.LIFE.com* to find out what it is.**

Page 64: **Office-Supply Shake-up** No. 1 (A2): Somebody has stolen a white paper clip. No. 2 (A5 to B5): A safety pin has invaded. No. 3 (B3): The plastic organizer has a black cross to bear. No. 4 (C2): Another white clip has entered the mix. No. 5 (C4): There's an extra green pushpin. No. 6 (C5): The top of a blue pushpin has turned red. No. 7 (D4 to E4): A green tack has changed to blue. No. 8 (E1 to E2): The yellow rubber band in the middle is gone. No. 9 (E4): Here's a sticking point—that green tack has lost its metal pin.

Page 66: **Neighborhood Watch** No. 1 (A1): Birds have landed on the pink chimney. No. 2 (A2): The red chimney is gone. No. 3 (A2 to B2): There's a denim jacket drying on the line. No. 4 (A5 to B5): The pipe has gained bright-orange fasteners. No. 5 (B5): The broom and mop handles have been stretched out. No. 6 (C2): Attention—there's no smoking here. No. 7 (C3): Flowers have bloomed on the plant. No. 8 (D3 to E1): It must be getting late—the building's shadow is lengthening. No. 9 (E2): A bunch of paving stones have merged.

Page 68: **Let the Sun Shine In**

4	6
5	1
3	2

Page 69: **Postcards From the Edge**

5	3
1	6
4	2

Page 70: **Eat Your Veggies!** No. 1 (A1 to A2): Those bananas sure have spoiled quickly. No. 2 (A5): There's more asparagus in the basket. No. 3 (A5 to B5): One carrot has gotten carried away. No. 4 (B3): The green pepper's stem has been snipped. No. 5 (B4 to B5): The apple has gone from green to red. No. 6 (C1): Someone's swapped an orange for a lemon. No. 7 (C1): Straw and all, the tomato juice is ready for drinking. No. 8 (C3): The orange juice has been refilled. No. 9 (D1 to E4): The cutting board has lost its tiles. No. 10 (D4): One extra berry couldn't hurt, could it?

Page 72: **Hats Off to You . . .** No. 1 (A1): The wooden pole appreciates the added support. No. 2 (A4 to A5): The tree has grown fuller. No. 3 (B1 to C1): The yellow ribbon now features polka dots. No. 4 (B3): There's an extra red bow on top of the hat. No. 5 (C3): The purple ribbon is longer. No. 6 (C3 to E3): The extra-long white ribbon has come out from behind the display. Nos. 7 and 8 (C5): That customer looks a little squirrelly. Also, a small red ribbon has been tied to the flowing dark-blue one. No. 9 (C5 to E5): The orange ribbon is now pink.

Page 73: **Jam-packed** No. 1 (A2): The directions on the sign have been reversed. No. 2 (A3 to A4): The skyline has sprouted one new building. No. 3 (B2): A white car is now in the pink. No. 4 (B2 to C2): Another red truck has squeezed into traffic. No. 5 (B4): The van has turned into a school bus full of what we're sure are unhappy kids. No. 6 (C1): Whoa—who brought the horse? No. 7 (C2 to D2): Someone's painted a logo on the delivery truck. No. 8 (C4 to C5): The blue station wagon is burning rubber. No. 9 (D1): The red car must have found a shortcut. No. 10 (D4): That couple have met their match. No. 11 (D5): More planters have been unloaded onto the median. No. 12 (E2): What a load of logs. **Did you find the secret bonus difference? If not, log on to *www.LIFE.com* to find out what it is.**

Page 74: **It Takes Two to Tango** No. 1 (A1 to B2): A little mood lighting might brighten up the room. No. 2 (B4): She's lost a strap. No. 3 (B5): The plant has grown taller. No. 4 (C2): An extra blue bottle now sits above the sofa. No. 5 (C3): Is that a stethoscope in his pocket, or is he just playing doctor? No. 6 (C4): His buttons have broken free. No. 7 (D1): The orange pillow has disappeared. No. 8 (E1): The sofa leg is longer. No. 9 (E3): The top of his shoe has turned pink. No. 10 (E4): An ankle tattoo? Sexy!

Page 76: **The Sky's the Limit** No. 1 (B1 to C2): A new tree has sprouted. No. 2 (B2): That roof is having a ball. No. 3 (B4): A rope has replaced one metal bar. No. 4 (C1 to C2): The slots now angle the other way. No. 5 (C3 to E3): The green pole is thicker. No. 6 (C5): A porthole is missing. No. 7 (D1): The slide is deeper. No. 8 (D2): A soccer ball has rolled into view. No. 9 (D2 to E2): The pole is now candy-striped—and, presumably, higher in carbs. No. 10 (D3): The flower has been plucked from her shoe. No. 11 (E4): The tan pole is sliding out of the frame.

Page 78: **Easy As Pie**

8	6	4
5	1	3
9	2	7

Page 79: **Bridal Arrangement**

3	7	4
9	6	2
5	1	8

Page 80: **Wake Up and Smell the Coffee** No. 1 (A2): The waitress's bow tie is askew. No. 2 (A4): The yellow-and-white lampshade has grown taller. No. 3 (A5 to B5): The wall has been repainted. No. 4 (B1): One caffeinated customer has stuck a pencil behind his ear. No. 5 (B1 to B2): What an, um, *interesting* collar your shirt has, ma'am. No. 6 (B2): Is it dark in here, or did a lamp disappear? No. 7 (B5): That coffee on the computer is going to void the warranty. No. 8 (C2 to E3): The cuffs and collar on his sweater have gotten darker. No. 9 (D1): Anybody seen his white stripe? No. 10 (D4): He needed a refill. Nos. 11 and 12 (E4): There's more lava in this lamp. And all the keyboard's keys are now gray.

Page 82: **Numbers Game** No. 1 (A2 to B2): The dangling red lace has been tucked in. No. 2 (A5): A wooden support is missing. No. 3 (B1): Whose mug is that? No. 4 (B4): Bob's very proprietary about his stuff. No. 5 (C3): Someone just loves L7. No. 6 (D5): That shoe's size must remain a mystery. No. 7 (E2): The heel has picked up a black stripe. No. 8 (E4): What a lovely shade of turquoise.

Page 83: **Paper Chase** No. 1 (A3): What time is it? No. 2 (B2): Dig that decoder ring. No. 3 (B3): His bow tie, ashamed of the disarray, has turned red. No. 4 (B4 to B5): The papers in the air have shrunk. No. 5 (C4): Fewer papers are on the floor. No. 6 (D2): The stamp handle has swelled to mammoth proportions. No. 7 (E2): A *b* has been stamped on the invoice. It must stand for "badly organized." No. 8 (E5): *Eek!* A mouse!

Page 84: **Leader of the Pack** No. 1 (A2 to B2): The bag strap has thickened. No. 2 (A5 to B5): The street painters have just passed through. No. 3 (B2): Mr. White Shirt's friendly helmet says "Hi!" No. 4 (B3 to B4): Take that Martian to your leader. No. 5 (B5): The number 3 has switched sides. No. 6 (C1): The rider has put down his visor. No. 7 (D1 to E2): Hey, you in front—no fair entering twice. No. 8 (D5): The bike's mirrors have grown. No. 9 (E3): The writing on the pavement has stretched forward.

Page 85: **Window Display** No. 1 (A1 to B1): The dome has grown. No. 2 (A2): The arch has gained some spires. No. 3 (A3 to B3): That dome looks a bit off-kilter. No. 4 (B4): The round windows are now diamond-shaped. No. 5 (B5): Two windows are missing. No. 6 (C1 to C3): Some stonework has been whitewashed. No. 7 (C3 to D3): The spire on the dome is extra-tall. No. 8 (D1 to D3): The arches above the window have turned green. No. 9 (E1): What's that in the window? No. 10 (E2): *Aww*, we heart you too.

Page 86: **Waiting for the Other Shoe to Drop** No. 1 (A1 to B1): The blooms' centers have turned yellow. No. 2 (A3 to C4): Where have all the white flowers gone? No. 3 (B2): That seam should be super-secure now. No. 4 (B5): The strap is green. No. 5 (C2 to C4): On sale now! No. 6 (C4): Those shoes are so lightweight, they're levitating. No. 7 (D2): A blue blossom has vanished. No. 8 (D5): One flower has become very blue. Cheer up. No. 9 (E5): A white flower has been added.

Page 88: **Make No Bones About It** The mural is extinct in image No. 3.

Page 89: **Life's a Beach** No. 5 is the odd one out. The red and green umbrellas have swapped places.

Page 90: **Queen for a Day** No. 1 (A5): A bottle of olive oil now sits on the top shelf. Nos. 2 and 3 (B1): That left cabinet is looking a little more *floral.* And who dares to leave a handprint on the palace walls? No. 4 (B2 to C2): A pink plate and glass fit for a queen have supplanted the fondue pot. No. 5 (B3): The handle has deserted the cabinet. No. 6 (C3): Some crown jewels have been added to her necklace. No. 7 (C4): The microwave's window has vanished. No. 8 (C4 to D4): Only a queen can get away with mismatched sleeves. No. 9 (C5): Another silly soap dispenser sits next to the microwave. No. 10 (D1 to E1): *X* marks the spot where an extra piece of wood has been inserted. No. 11 (D2): The center of one place mat has doubled in size. No. 12 (E4 to E5): The tiled wall now extends to the palace floor.

Page 92: **Don't Shelve This One** No. 1 (A2): The white can now reads COFFEE COFFEE COFFEE. No. 2 (A3 to A4): Let's double up on that tasty Royal Dutch coffee. No. 3 (B1 to C2): The sage has shuffled off, but we have double the thyme (and ginger) on our hands. No. 4 (B2 to B5): The yellow sign has gotten longer. No. 5 (B4): A small red tin has been stacked on top of the baking soda. Nos. 6 and 7 (B5 to C5): The face on the blue box has mysteriously disappeared. And the Canada Dry bottle is tilting to the left. No. 8 (C1): The man on the red tin is standing on his head. No. 9 (C3): The silver elephants are larger. No. 10 (D2): The Saltina Biscuit tin has grown taller. No. 11 (D3 to E3): A lady has replaced the military man. No. 12 (D3 to E4): The red Sultan Emery tin has faded to green. No. 13 (E1): The saltine tin has lost its CRACKERS. No. 14 (E4): EMERY is now EMORY. **Did you find the secret bonus difference? If not, log on to *www.LIFE.com* to find out what it is.**

[EXPERT]

Page 96: **Seeing Spots?** No. 1 (A2 to B2): The spot above her front leg has grown. Nos. 2 and 3 (B3): This cow's day is looking up. And her hooves have turned white. No. 4 (B4): This calf has *moo*ved closer to the camera. No. 5 (B5): She seems udderly lost. No. 6 (C1): The brown patch of grass has been revived. No. 7 (C3): Elsie has a shorter rope around her neck. No. 8 (E4): That bovine is *wide* awake. No. 9 (E5): And she's swinging her tail.

Page 98: **No Downtime** No. 1 (A2): The binders on the top shelf now lean left. No. 2 (A3 to A4): The bright-orange books are taller. No. 3 (A4): A red volume has swapped places with a yellow one. No. 4 (B1): The dots on the black binders have moved up. No. 5 (B5): The coffee cup has shimmied over. No. 6 (C2 to D2): Someone has taped up the box more securely. Nos. 7 and 8 (C3): The purple cushion has shrunk, and the oak drawer behind it has gained a new handle on things. No. 9 (C4 to D4): His glasses are missing! No. 10 (D5): The black table has an extra leg to stand on.

Page 99: **Everything Must Go** No. 1 (A1): The second floor of the house has been extended. No. 2 (A3): Another cabinet has been added to the pile. No. 3 (A4): The windows on the garage door have been removed. No. 4 (B2): More black and white plastic seats have been stacked up. No. 5 (C3 to C4): Another layer of orange cushions has been tacked onto that wacky sofa. (Maybe they're on loan from the puzzle on page 98.) No. 6 (C4 to D4): Two yellow drawers have merged into one. No. 7 (D1): Okay, who took the silverware handles? No. 8 (D3): The girl's dress is longer. And cuter. No. 9 (D4 to D5): Two drums, twice the fun. No. 10 (E2): That toolbox up front needs to get a grip. No. 11 (E5): The oven rack beneath the table is gone.

Page 100: **Welcome to the Dollhouse** No. 1 (A1): The point on the gold hat is longer. No. 2 (A4): The gold trim adorning the pink hat has been snipped. No. 3 (B3): She's put on lipstick to match her neighbor on the right. Copycat. No. 4 (B5): Her eyebrows have been plucked. Nos. 5 and 6 (D1): A blue stripe on that jester's hat has expanded, and her lips have turned green. No. 7 (D4): A silver bar has been added to the rack. No. 8 (D4 to E4): Is it a hassle to wear such a big tassel? No. 9 (D5): She's dolled herself up with some blush. No. 10 (E3): Her gold pin has grown. **Did you find the secret bonus difference? If not, log on to *www.LIFE.com* to find out what it is.**

Page 102: **Don't Paint Yourself Into a Corner** In photo No. 2, the paint in the cup at top right is blue instead of red.

Page 103: **Fabric Fiesta!** The wares in picture No. 5 are not like the rest. At the bottom of the blue blanket, there are now two rows of the bright-green pattern.

Page 104: **Bubbling Over** No. 1 (A4): Her hat has a new crown. No. 2 (B2): The champagne champ's tank top has morphed into a muscle shirt. No. 3 (B4): Weigh the anchor—it seems to have gained some heft. No. 4 (C1 to D1): A red flower on her dress has turned purple. Nos. 5 and 6 (C3): The blonde's been to the manicurist. Meanwhile, you know, sometimes a cigar is not a cigar. It's a carrot. No. 7 (C4): Her bracelet has cloned itself. No. 8 (D2): Refill? No. 9 (D4): The skipper has lost a gold button. No. 10 (E2 to E3): The grapes have crowded out the strawberries. No. 11 (E5): The chair has more slats.

Page 106: **Don't Go Nuts** No. 1 (A1 to B2): The gold crescent is thicker. No. 2 (A3): He's nabbing some shut-eye. No. 3 (A4 to B4): His hat is seeing stars. No. 4 (A5): The red feather is tilting right. No. 5 (B3): A dot now bisects his hat's stripe. No. 6 (B4): His chapeau's gold ball has rolled away. No. 7 (C1): The lines on his jacket have been extended. No. 8 (C1 to C2): Hope he has a good dentist. No. 9 (D2 to D3): Things are looking brighter for that triangle. No. 10 (D3 to D4): The lavender dots now sit atop his mustache. No. 11 (E2): His jacket has picked up some buttons. No. 12 (E5): His white legs are now yellow.

Page 108: **Congratulations Are in Order** No. 1 (A3): The balcony has lost a pillar. No. 2 (B3 to C3): A butterfly brooch has landed on her dress. Nos. 3 and 4 (C1): The mother of the bride looks pretty in pink. And the button on her jacket is now gold. No. 5 (C5): Another fern has joined the bouquet. No. 6 (D2): That dress has become truly fit for a flower girl. No. 7 (E1 to E2): Her basket is shorter. No. 8 (E3 to E5): Happy guests have tossed more rose petals. **Did you find the secret bonus difference? If not, log on to *www.LIFE.com* to find out what it is.**

Page 110: **Slightly Off-key** No. 1 (A1): A cellist has grown taller. No. 2 (B2): Both covers of the sheet music are showing. No. 3 (B4): Has someone discovered hair in a can? No. 4 (B5): A copy of the sheet music has been relabeled. Maybe they're switching to Bach. No. 5 (C1): The back of the cellist's chair has widened. No. 6 (C2): A stand has left the room. The question is, was the movement adagio or allegro? Nos. 7 and 8 (C4): One of the three trumpet stands on the floor is gone, and the musician has changed his sock. No. 9 (D5): Some sheet music is missing. No. 10 (E1): The silver bar has grown. No. 11 (E5): The tom-tom mount on the bass drum has been extended. **Did you find the secret bonus difference? If not, log on to *www.LIFE.com* to find out what it is.**

Page 112: **There Goes the Neighborhood**

8	2	9
3	10	1
11	5	12
4	7	6

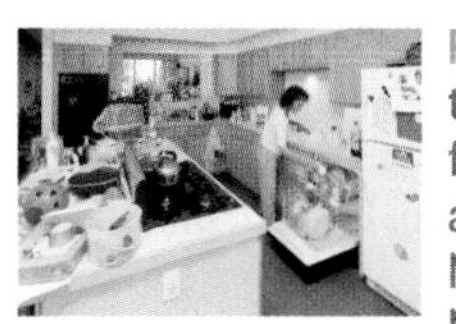

Page 113: **Whatever Floats Your Boat**

11	9	2
3	4	10
8	5	7
1	12	6

Page 114: **Counter Intelligence** No. 1 (A1 to A2): The cabinets above the oven are now family-size. No. 2 (B3): Another jar has appeared. No. 3 (B4): Coffee's ready. No. 4 (B4): There's more soda on the counter. No. 5 (C1): The jack-o'-lantern got a nose job. No. 6 (C2): The kettle's handle is higher. No. 7 (D2): A ball on the bucket has lost its stripes. No. 8 (D2 to D3): Tiled countertops are so last year, anyway. No. 9 (D5): The magnet's colors have flipped. No. 10 (E3): Here's some electrifying news: The socket has shifted.

Page 116: **Candy Is Dandy** No. 1 (A3): *Mmm.* Bonus red hot. No. 2 (A4): That yellow gummy bear looks mischievous. No. 3 (B2 to C3): The long multicolored lolly picked up a white stripe. No. 4 (C3): The yellow-and-white–striped candy has gone the way of the 10-cent Hershey bar. No. 5 (C3 to D3): The orange gum ball has lost face. No. 6 (D2): Someone's doubled up on blue candy. No. 7 (D4 to E4): The black-and-white candy has reversed its stripes. No. 8 (D5 to E5): The gummy frog has gotten bigger. No. 9 (E1): A banana has changed direction. Maybe it's going to split. No. 10 (E3 to E4): Is that licorice growing?

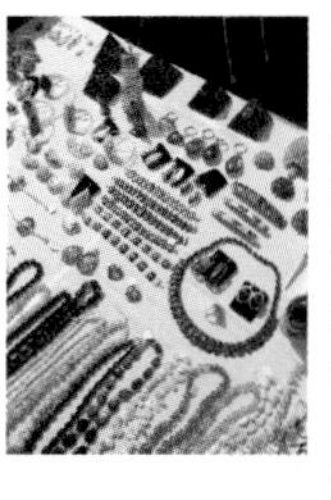

Page 118: **Leave No Stone Unturned** No. 1 (B3): A heart-shaped key chain has swapped spots with a teardrop one. (Is there a subliminal message here?) No. 2 (B4): One key ring has grown. Nos. 3 and 4 (B5): One amber pyramid has moved away from its neighbor, while the yellow brooch has been replaced by a brown one. No. 5 (C1): A thief took off with some silver. No. 6 (C2 to C3): The bracelet's pattern has been remixed. No. 7 (C4): An earring is upside down. No. 8 (C4 to C5): Another barrette has arrived. No. 9 (D1): The light-amber necklace has moved down. No. 10 (D3 to D4): Larger stones have cropped up in the center of the necklace. Lovely, don't you think?

Page 120: **Caught Red-handed** No. 1 (A3): The chair back has been reinforced. No. 2 (B3): The scarlet *A* has turned green. No. 3 (C2): Suzanne has become Suzanna. No. 4 (C3): The center tin has a bit more blue paint. No. 5 (C4): A blue *P* has rotated. No. 6 (C5): The front of that boy's shirt is now solid red. No. 7 (D3): A red *D* has been *D*-leted. No. 8 (E1): The table support has widened. No. 9 (E2): The green-and-red *N* has flipped upside down over the red splotch. No. 10 (E5): Yes, that's a yellow sponge on the floor. *Y* do you ask?

Page 122: **Make History** No. 1 (A1): Two stars have shot off the flag. No. 2 (A5 to B5): The chalkboard has been rubbed out. No. 3 (B2): The first *R* in REGULATOR is all stretched out. No. 4 (B4): In the classroom photo, one white box on the blackboard has vanished. No. 5 (B5): The scroll has grown longer. No. 6 (C3): George Washington is going for a new sporty-casual look. No. 7 (C4 to C5): Teddy Roosevelt has replaced Honest Abe in the frame (but not in our hearts). No. 8 (D2): The lid has turned green. No. 9 (D3): The bell's handle is larger. No. 10 (D4): The bat handle has been taped up. No. 11 (D5 to E5): The girl in the frame has switched sides. No. 12 (E2): So *that's* where the pencil went.

Page 124: ***Pa-Rum-Pum-Pum-Pum*** No. 1 (A2 to B2): The man with the umbrella has stepped inside. No. 2 (B2): The drummer boy's hat decoration is now red and blue, not white and blue. No. 3 (B4): The drumstick has taken a new angle. No. 4 (B4 to C4): Who's the new kid? No. 5 (B5): Her coat has gained a button. No. 6 (C5): He's pulled up his strap. No. 7 (D2 to E3): Her drum has lost its red stripes. No. 8 (D3): His uniform is no longer uniform—his red cuff has turned blue. No. 9 (E1): Wait till her mom sees those grass stains.

ANSWERS

Page 125: **Dress Dilemma** No. 1 (A1): The mural has been extended to the left. No. 2 (A4 to C5): The red and orange dresses have switched places. No. 3 (B1): The striped dress has picked up an extra brown band. No. 4 (B5): There's something fishier about that red dress. No. 5 (C1): A yin-and-yang symbol is now a sunburst. No. 6 (C2): The dark dress has become more modest (nice cap sleeves). No. 7 (C3): Are maxiskirts back? No. 8 (D2): A flower has been added to the orange dress. No. 9 (D4): The bare midriff has been covered up. No. 10 (D4 to E4): A new line of white flowers has sprouted on the orange dress. No. 11 (D4 to E5): The flames are getting higher. That is so hot!

Page 126: **Unnatural Selection** No. 1 (A2): The larger horseshoe crab has shrunk. No. 2 (A3): The crab's middle leg is gone. No. 3 (B4 to B5): More butterflies have fluttered in. Nos. 4 and 5 (C3): One knob on the video monitor is askew. Plus, the black lobster's tail is longer. Nos. 6 and 7 (C5): A maple leaf has infiltrated the bug case, while the purple sea creatures on the screen have ballooned. Nos. 8 and 9 (D1): The anteater had to turn away from the fumes of the freshly painted shelf bracket. No. 10 (D1 to E1): The picture has faded to black. Nos. 11 and 12 (D2): Another spider has joined the gang, but he won't be among his pals for long if that armadillo's tail keeps growing. No. 13 (D4): A lobster has morphed into a sea horse. No. 14 (D4 to E5): The model of the insect leg on the table has tilted up. No. 15 (E2): A table leg has broken off.

[GENIUS]

Page 130: **Blown Out of Proportion** No. 1 (A4 to B4): A tree branch has been trimmed. No. 2 (B2): A beach ball's yellow dot has blown up. No. 3 (C1 to D1): The dots on the red-and-white beach ball have clustered together. No. 4 (D2): Her ring has jumped one finger over. Nos. 5, 6, and 7 (D5): A Christmas tree on the candy-cane balloon has grown up, and the giraffe's looking spottier. Meanwhile, Minnie Mouse has ditched pink for orange. No. 8 (E1): The duck's foot has grown larger. Hope it's not gout. No. 9 (E2 to E3): The bear's looking left. No. 10 (E4): The mouse's black tail has been curled in the opposite direction.

Page 131: **Signs of the Times** No. 1 (A3 to B3): The turkey's tail is now scalloped. No. 2 (A4): The cups have moved up. No. 3 (A5): The ampersand on HARDY & CO. has flipped. No. 4 (C1): The red sign has double the swirl. No. 5 (C1 to C3): The couple have grown taller. No. 6 (C4 to D5): The sextant has grown. No. 7 (C5): The rooster is feeling footloose. Sorry, foot*less*. No. 8 (D1): The world has turned upside down! Well, the globe has, anyway. No. 9 (D2): His ascot has lost its polka dots. That's a crime in some countries. No. 10 (D3 to D4): The golfer has put on longer pants.

Page 132: **Which One Changed Its Stripes?** Photo No. 5 has been altered. A hot-pink band in the center of one earring has turned orange.

Page 133: **Lend Us Your Ears** Image No. 1 has the nonconforming cob. The whitish cob (third from right)has an extra purple kernel. It's 12 kernels from the bottom on the third row from the right. You didn't really find that, did you?

Page 134: **Housing Boom** No. 1 (A4): Renovations have left this building with one less window. No. 2 (B1): A yellow house has been painted turquoise. No. 3 (B3): Another chimney has popped up on the black roof. No. 4 (B4 to B5): The green chimney has skipped town. No. 5 (C1): The shady section of the gray building has acquired another window. No. 6 (C2): The green pole has grown taller. No. 7 (C5): The building now has just one balcony. Nos. 8 and 9 (D5): The round window on the red building is gone. Below that, the windows on the yellow building are wider and have more panes. No. 10 (E1): Part of the sign has shifted left.

Page 136: **Closet Chaos** No. 1 (A4): The yellow-and-blue object atop the closet has moved to the right. No. 2 (B2): One yellow strap has grown longer. No. 3 (B5 to C5): A paint-splattered bag deserves paint-splattered handles. No. 4 (C3): The blue jacket's yellow piping is now dotted. Nos. 5 and 6 (D3): A bear on the sweater is looking skyward. And the red tote has lost its gold dragonfly. No. 7 (D5): The basket has fewer holes. No. 8 (E1): The black stripe on one of the yellow galoshes has thickened. No. 9 (E3): Someone has swiped the shoelace. No. 10 (E5): One red Wellington has ditched its handle.

Page 138: **No Bunny Slope**

6	12	13	11
15	9	16	8
2	14	1	5
7	4	10	3

Page 139: **Like Mother, Like Daughter**

11	9	5	15
1	8	12	13
3	14	6	4
2	10	16	7

Page 140: **Special Delivery** No. 1 (A2): The dog's tail has drooped. No. 2 (B1 to C1): The New Zealand stamp has been flipped. No. 3 (B3): The butterfly's right hind wing has been lengthened at the tip. No. 4 (B4): The weight lifter is sporting a powerfully green getup. Nos. 5 and 6 (C2): One of the purple microbes has inched up. And the Italian gentleman to its right now has a groovy handlebar mustache. No. 7 (C4): The green Indian stamp is now straight-edged. Nos. 8 and 9 (C5): Another flag has been hoisted onto the hot air balloon, and on the Suriname stamp, the bird's long tail feather is missing. Nos. 10 and 11 (D3): TOGO has been renamed TOGA. Below that, the Canadian stamp now costs 6 cents. Inflation. No. 12 (E3): The horn on the orange stamp has diminished. No. 13 (E4): The *L* on the LIONS stamp has been set in an Old English font.

Page 142: **Masked Madness** No. 1 (A3): The gap between his teeth has moved to the right. No. 2 (A4): Mr. Green's ears are no longer pink. No. 3 (B2): There's a longer cut etched into his cheek. Looks painful. Nos. 4 and 5 (B4): Mr. Green has stuck his tongue way out. That horse below him isn't licked, but he does have longer lines around his alert eyes. No. 6 (C1 to D1): The striped yellow mask has vamoosed. No. 7 (C5): That bird still has a hole in his head, but at least it has shrunk a bit. No. 8 (D1): The human mask now has a red tip on his nose. Maybe his name is Rudolph. No. 9 (D4): That anteater's right eye has blackened slightly. No. 10 (E4): The yarn tangle has been straightened out. No. 11 (E5): The pupil on the far right has shrunk.

Page 144: **Where to Begin?** No. 1 (A1 to A2): The printer's out of paper. No. 2 (A2): Someone has switched on the lava lamp. Cue up the Pink Floyd. No. 3 (A4): Check out the new height of the headboard's left post. No. 4 (A5): An extra red pepper has appeared. Spicy! Nos. 5 and 6 (B1): The window shade has dropped. But the cabinet's doorknob has moved up. No. 7 (B3): The phone antenna has vanished. That explains the bad reception. No. 8 (C1 to D1): If you see a one-legged man wearing a black shoe, this guy would like a word with him. Nos. 9 and 10 (C2): The chair's support has turned black. And is it time for another cup of coffee? No. 11 (C3 to C4): The pillowcase now sports blue stripes. No. 12 (D1): The music stand has grown an extra leg. No. 13 (D2): The blue and pink papers on the floor have switched places. No. 14 (D3): The book's bar code has been relocated. No. 15 (D4): He has unsheathed the box of Peeps. Heaven help us all. No. 16 (E1): The CD player is now playing. What are the odds it's *Dark Side of the Moon*? No. 17 (E2): The yarn is snaking into the drawer. Nos. 18 and 19 (E2 to E3): The hair gel has flipped and rolled onto its side, perhaps to eye that added pocket change. No. 20 (E5): The 8 on the poster is now a big fat 0.

[LIFE CLASSICS]

Page 148: **Who Reset the Table?** No. 1 (A1 to B2): The artwork lineup has been shuffled. No. 2 (A3 to C3): The shadow on the door has vanished. No. 3 (B4 to C4): The doorknob now covers the lock. No. 4 (C2 to C3): Her new belt completes the outfit. Nos. 5, 6, and 7 (D2): The black candy dishes are multiplying. Over on the table, one cup has been filled, and another has misplaced its saucer. No. 8 (E2 to E3): The pattern on the plate went *poof.* No. 9 (E4): And a serving spoon did too.

Page 150: **One-Stop Shopping** No. 1 (A2 to C4): The banner no longer has a white border. No. 2 (A3): The stone decoration above one window has gotten bigger. No. 3 (A4): The exclamation point after AND JUSTICE FOR ALL has fallen off. No. 4 (B1): An extra gargoyle now guards the building. No. 5 (B4): The shield has dropped a stripe. No. 6 (B5): That column looks even fancier. No. 7 (C1 to D1): A poster has grown up. No. 8 (C5): SNOW has replaced SHOW. No. 9 (D5): The car's rear panel now has a handle. No. 10 (E1): The traffic line has gone from solid to dotted. No. 11 (E4): Grandpa's picked up another bag of goodies.

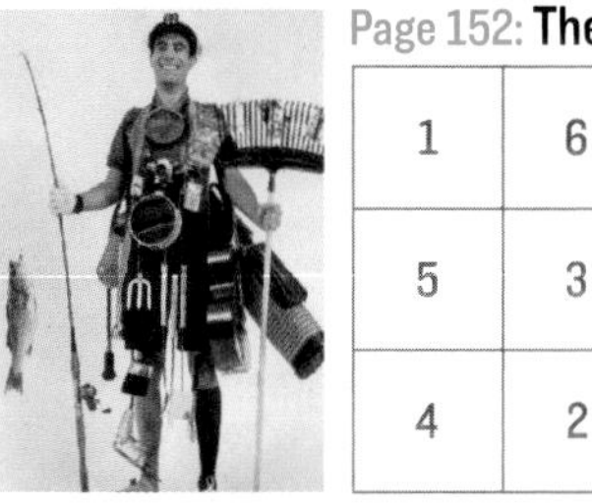

Page 152: **The Man Who Has Everything**

1	6
5	3
4	2

Page 153: **Time to Tidy Up**

4	6
1	5
2	3

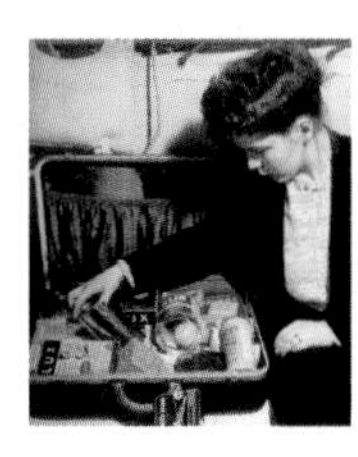

Page 154: **Bon Voyage** No. 1 (A1 to A2): The lettering has been darkened. No. 2 (A4): Extra rope is securing the tarp. No. 3 (B4 to D5): That's a lovely new shirt. No. 4 (C2 to D2): Her jacket now extends over her sleeve. No. 5 (D1): An *E* has been added to LUX. How luxurious. No. 6 (D3): The bottom of the can is no longer reflective. No. 7 (E1 to E4): The suitcase has been unbuckled permanently.

ANSWERS

Page 156: **Get Back on Track** No. 1 (A2 to A3): His hat has gained a black band. No. 2 (A3 to A4): The sign now reads EAST. No. 3 (B1): Looks like they worked past sundown. That's dedication. No. 4 (B5): Two conductors have been dropped from the list. No. 5 (C2): Did she tell a lie? Her nose is growing. No. 6 (C5): An extra piece of paper has been tacked up. No. 7 (D3 to E3): The desk drawer now has two knobs. No. 8 (D3 to D5): The cord has disappeared. No. 9 (E5): The desk has become shallower.

Page 158: **Bumper Crop** No. 1 (A2 to B3): Three panels have merged into one. No. 2 (A4 to A5): A cross has been placed inside the trellis's diamond center. No. 3 (B5 to C5): The grass has overtaken the path. No. 4 (C1): The crate has collected an extra cabbage. Slawtastic! No. 5 (C3): She has let out the hem of her skirt. No. 6 (C4): Someone has labeled the lettuce crate. Nos. 7 and 8 (C4 to D5): That onion crate has mushroomed, and it's acquired a taste for squash. No. 9 (D4): The basket has been repaired.

Page 160: **She Couldn't Put It Down** No. 1 (A2): The bottle cap has changed color. No. 2 (B1 to C2): Her hair has grown fuller. Is she using a volumizer? Nos. 3, 4, and 5 (B4): In the advertisement, another olive has appeared in the glass. Next to it, someone has snatched a pint. Plus, the 10-cent tag has moved one magazine to the left. No. 6 (C2): Her mole has migrated. No. 7 (C5): One wedding dress has a higher neckline. So traditional. No. 8 (D4): The Yankees emblem has hopped to the left on his uniform. No. 9 (D5): *Blue Book*'s logo has sunk. **Did you find the secret bonus difference? If not, log on to *www.LIFE.com* to find out what it is.**

Page 162: **The Party's Over?** No. 1 (A1 to B1): It's curtains for that curtain. No. 2 (B1 to C2): The chair's back bars are higher. No. 3 (B3 to B4): One chair has double the back support. No. 4 (B5): One of the horse's handles is longer. No. 5 (C1 to C2): A junior architect has added a wooden triangle to a column. No. 6 (C2): HAPPY BIRTHDAY has been erased from the tablecloth. No. 7 (C4): Another peg has been fastened to the top of the elevator toy. No. 8 (C5 to D5): The baby carriage now has extra racing stripes. *Vroom!* Nos. 9 and 10 (D3): Says MILK on it—must be milk. And is one tub of ice cream melting? Nos. 11 and 12 (D4): Another clown ball has rolled in for the party, and the semi's roof has been blackened. No. 13 (E1): The train's rope has grown longer. No. 14 (E2): The engine's second wheel has rolled away. No. 15 (E3): Would the owner of the black truck report to the playroom? Your headlights are on.

So . . . how'd you do?

[LOOK FOR THE NEXT LIFE PICTURE PUZZLE BOOK IN AUGUST 2007!]